AF840898

Black Oedipus

Coloniality and the Foreclosure of Gender and Race

Rita Segato

Translated by
Ramsey McGlazer

1968

Cover Image:

Anonymous.
Nhozinho no colo da mucama [Little Boy on the Maid's Lap].
Oil on canvas, 0,55 x 0,44m.

Museu Imperial/ IBRAM
R. da Imperatriz, 220 – Centro, Petrópolis – RJ, 25610-320

https://museuimperial.museus.gov

'O édipo brasileiro: A dupla negação de gênero e raça' by Rita Segato was first published in Portuguese by the Department of Anthropology of the University of Brasília, Brazil, in 2006.

An enlarged and revised version was published in Spanish as 'El Edipo brasilero: Doble negación de género y raza' in M. L. Femenías, *Perfiles del feminismo Iberoamericano* (Buens Aires: Catálogos, 2007).

An earlier version of the present translation is included in Rita Segato, *The Critique of Coloniality: Eight Essays*, trans. by Ramsey McGlazer (Abingdon: Routledge, 2022).

First published in English 2026 by 1968 Press

Translation © Ramsey McGlazer

ISBN: 9781919601960 (pbk & ebk)

Printed by Clays Ltd., Bungay

1968 Press, London

important
little
books in
psychoanalysis

Important Little Books in Psychoanalysis

Series edited by
Raluca Soreanu, Lizaveta van Munsteren
and the FREEPSY collective

Contents

A Preface in Three Scenes

Ramsey McGlazer

Scene 1

Sometimes, when Sigmund Freud falls asleep, he dreams of dumplings. 'Tired and hungry after a journey, I went to bed', he remembers in *The Interpretation of Dreams*, 'and the major vital needs began to announce their presence in my sleep'.[1] The hungry Freud dreams that he walks into a hotel kitchen only to be told that he has to wait: the dumplings that 'the hostess of the inn' is preparing aren't ready yet.[2] What follows is an elaborate dream, one that leads to an even more baroque analysis involving overcoats, Turkish patterns, the three Fates, and many proper names. Briefly, Freud's associations also return him to the scene of the infant's first feeding: 'love and hunger, I reflected, meet at a woman's breast'. Here Freud takes a sudden turn from the aphoristic to the anecdotal: 'a young man who was a great admirer of feminine beauty was talking once—so the story went—of the good-looking wet nurse who had suckled him when he was a baby: "I'm sorry", he remarked, "that I didn't make better use of my opportunity". I was in the habit of quoting this anecdote to explain the factor of "deferred action" [*Nachträglichkeit*] in the psychoneuroses'.[3]

If this Freudian story sounds familiar, that may be because it's one of Jean Laplanche's favourite examples of *Nachträglichkeit* or what he calls 'afterwardsness'. More than once, Laplanche returns to this moment in Freud's dream book. How exactly, he asks, does the anecdote 'explain' or distil the dynamics of the key concept that James Strachey translates as 'deferred action'? At first, Laplanche notes, it seems as if there are two available ways to understand the story. Either we can join the man, who, in his 'retrospective fantasizing', 'reinterprets the function of breast feeding in terms of his present situation', emphasising the erotic pleasure he would derive, as an adult, if he were in the baby's place; *or* we can return to Freud's own teachings on infantile sexuality and see the baby's suckling as already an erotically charged experience.[4]

But, for Laplanche, these two interpretive paths—which he calls the 'hermeneutic' and the 'deterministic', or the 'retroactive' and the 'progressive'—are unsatisfying. Both are 'equally centered on the subject: that is, the infantile subject, and the adult subject'.[5] Both interpretations, in other words, revolve around His Majesty the Baby. 'What Freud scotomises or does not wish to see in this example is simply [...] the wet-nurse', Laplanche concludes. His discussion of the implications of this blind spot is worth quoting at length:

> Here Freud ignores the wet-nurse and her own sexuality. He has completely forgotten his [early] seduction theory, and he does not take into account the pleasure of the seductive nurse or mother which will be central to the Leonardo study. He treats the breast as an *object* for the infant, and not as an erotic zone for the nurse. So if one introduces a third term into this scene—that is, the nurse and her own sexuality, which is no doubt vaguely sensed by the baby—then it is no longer possible to consider afterwardsness as a combination of two opposed terms. The third term, then, is what is passed to the infant from the adult: the nurse's *message* to the infant.[6]

This is 'the implantation of the enigmatic message' that it will be the subject's task to translate and retranslate, interminably.[7]

Scene 2

At a distance, Laplanche's rejoinder to Freud anticipates Rita Segato's remarkable *Black Oedipus*. Or rather, we can read Laplanche's work and Segato's alongside one another as an 'exercise in reciprocal exegesis'. In another book, Segato uses this phrase to name the kind of conversation that she stages, a tense exchange between psychanalysis and anthropology.[8] In *Black Oedipus* the conversation continues, and what results is paradoxically at once a provincialisation and a deepening of psychoanalytic theory.

Implicit in Laplanche's critique of Freud is the claim that his forgetting of—his failure to see—the nurse is overdetermined, a product of both patriarchal and class privilege. Although Laplanche refers to 'the seductive nurse or mother', as if the difference between the two were negligible (and this is interesting in light of Segato's argument about kinship in *Black Oedipus*), he also calls attention to the class difference that separates the analyst from the hired help whose pleasure is so easily set aside. This nurse 'is hardly anything more than the support of an object without enigma, an object to be consumed'.[9] To be sure, this could be a characterisation of any mother, seen in the misogynist imaginary that Segato analyses as a mere source of sustenance and emotional support for her baby. But Laplanche's sentence is especially salient as a description of the nursing nanny, a purveyor of breastmilk for consumption whose livelihood depends on her willingness to appear to be compliant, undemanding, and 'without enigma'.

In *Black Oedipus,* Segato shows that, in and implicitly beyond Brazil, this figure is racialised.[10] The nurse's exploitation shores up the racist, colonial, modern, masculinist order. What Laplanche calls Freud's scotomisation of the wet-nurse, Segato recasts as both this nurse's 'sacrifice' and her foreclosure. This alters our understanding of the problem, its site, its scale, its social extent, and its violence: it's not just that, despite the prevalence of her labour, the black *babá* cannot be acknowledged or even privately avowed in, let alone treated as kin within, white Brazilian families. More consequentially, her participation in the 'primal scene' of breastfeeding—her role in the shaping of psychic life—cannot even be seen. It remains unnameable, imperceptible, 'expelled in advance, before an attachment to it can be experienced', as Segato writes.

Here, though, we come to a crucial turn in the argument of *Black Oedipus.* The wet-nurse remains invisible to Euro-descendant Brazilians, *but then, through the medium of painting, the* babá *becomes visible to Segato, a Euro-descendant mother raising a child in Brazil.* Does this disclosure somehow follow from her status as 'foreigner'? Does her capacity to see relate to her training as an anthropologist, or to the fact of travelling with a group of 'professors of anthropology'? We cannot be sure. What we do know is that a painting in the Imperial Palace at Petrópolis, a dual portrait, suddenly interpellates Segato. It stops her short, trips her up, slows her down. And, for a time at least, it separates her from the group, from her colleagues and traveling companions. In Laplanche's terms, the painting 'reopen[s] the dimension of alterity' for Segato, and it reactivates the enigma.[11] It seduces her, in other words, the way Laplanche's 'adult' seduces the child.[12] It makes her an addressee, assigns her a mission, imposes a task: the task of working out its meaning, interpreting and reinterpreting its message. Laplanche's other name for this effort is 'translation'.

Black Oedipus is such an intricate and powerful text at the level of content that it is easy to miss this feature of its form: the essay is a record of repeated acts of translation. It attests to an ongoing, processual, and ruminative response to an aesthetic object: a painting that, out of time, interrupts and reorients the anthropologist. Importantly, the epiphany is not once-and-done; it recurs, taking place first in Petrópolis, then again in a library in Gainesville, Florida, of all places. Here, uncannily, Segato comes across a reproduction of the painting that, in an *après-coup*, a scene of 'afterwardsness' or deferred action, again assails her. The portrait again prompts a search for answers that prove elusive. The painting's subjects, the language of their intimacy, and their surprising gazes lead her to formulate questions differently. At first suddenly, then gradually, the painting thus reorganises her perception. *Black Oedip*us seeks to reorganise ours.

Scene 3

But what, if anything, do Laplanche's remarks on the endless retranslation of the enigmatic message have to do with the practice of interlingual translation? Honestly, I do not know, although, having had the privilege of translating Segato's prose for several years now, I have spent a long time thinking about the question.[13] The publication of *Black Oedipus* as a standalone book has given me the rare opportunity to retranslate a previously published translation, and I have been grateful for the chance to correct old errors, address infelicities, and smooth over distracting rough edges.

I have written elsewhere about the challenges and rewards of translating Segato's complex, tonally wide-ranging, and often-playful prose.[14] Returning to her Spanish again, I have been reminded of all that makes it distinctive: the enormous breadth, formidable erudition, and incredible intellectual ambition; the rich texture of references; the weaving-together of discourses and the reframing of debates. No matter how many times I reread *Black Oedipus*, I remain 'overwhelmed', like Segato when she finds herself 'face to face' with the 'overwhelming' aesthetic object that is the painting in Petrópolis. When the painting arrests her, when it 'strikes' her, more than once, it does so with such force that she comes to see the effort to understand it as what Freud might have called a 'major vital need'. *Black Oedipus* puts readers in touch with the urgency of that need, that desire. In the translation that follows, I have tried to channel at least some of the energy of an aesthetic encounter that kept the author up at night.

Notes

1 Sigmund Freud, *The Interpretation of Dreams* [1899/1900], trans. by James Strachey, in *The Standard Edition of the Complete Psychological Works of Sigmund Freud, Volume IV (1900):* The Interpretation of Dreams *(First Part)*, ed. by James Strachey, with Anna Freud, assisted by Alix Strachey and Alan Tyson, 24 vols (London: Vintage, 2001) IV, p.204.

2 ibid. p.204.

3 ibid. pp.204-205.

4 Jean Laplanche, 'Notes on Afterwardsness', in *Essays on Otherness* [1999], ed. by John Fletcher, trans. by Luke Thurston and others (London: Routledge, 2005) p.268.

5 ibid.

6 ibid. pp.268-269.

7 ibid. p.269.

8 Rita Segato, 'La célula violenta que Lacan no vió', in *Las estructuras elementales de la violencia: Ensayos sobre género entre la antropología, el psicoanálisis y los derechos humanos* (Bernal: Universidad Nacional de Quilmes, 2003) p.101. This chapter on the psychic life of patriarchy forms an important companion to *Black Oedipus*; the two texts can be read as a kind of diptych.

9 Jean Laplanche, 'Time and the Other', in *Essays on Otherness*, p.262.

10 For another important study of the relationship between racialisation and the withholding of enigma, see Antonio Viego, *Dead Subjects: Toward a Politics of Loss in Latino Studies* (Durham and London: Duke University Press, 2007).

11 See Jean Laplanche, 'Transference: Its Provocation by the Analyst', in *Essays on Otherness*, p.233.

12 On why Laplanche refers to the 'adult' rather than the 'parent', see Jean Laplanche, *New Foundations for Psychoanalysis*, trans. by David Macey (Oxford: Basil Blackwell, 1989) p.124. His arguments for displacing the emphasis on biological kinship are obliquely related to Segato's account of the wet nurse's central role in the infant's psychic life.

13 I began translating Segato's work for the inaugural issue of *Critical Times*, which featured her important essay 'A Manifesto in Four Themes', *Critical Times* 1.1 (2018) 198-211, https://doi.org/10.1215/26410478-1.1.198. Since then, I have translated two of Segato's essay collections: *The Critique of Coloniality: Eight Essays* (Abingdon: Routledge, 2022), and *The War Against Women* (Cambridge: Polity, 2025).

14 Ramsey McGlazer, 'Stowaways: On Translating Rita Segato', *Berkeley Review of Latin American Studies* (2023) 2-6.

Introduction

Maria Ribeiro[1]

'O édipo brasileiro: A dupla negação de gênero e raça' by Rita Segato was first published in Portuguese by the Department of Anthropology of the University of Brasília, Brazil, in 2006. An enlarged and revised version was published in Spanish as 'El edipo brasilero' in M. L. Femenias, *Perfiles de pensamiento iberoamericano,* Catálogos, Buenos Aires, in 2007. After this date, Segato changed the title from 'Brazilian Oedipus' to 'Black Oedipus', and this is how it was republished in both Spanish and Portuguese thereafter. Its argument on the specificities of Brazilian motherhood is supported by a historical, anthropological, and psychic investigation that converges on the 'soothing veneer' of the enslaved Black woman—a discursive strategy concerned with a palliation of the deadly choices made within the colonial order for non-white populations, particularly Indigenous and Black people. In 1980, the Black Brazilian intellectual Lélia Gonzalez, in dialogue with the white French psychoanalyst Jacques Lacan, called the 'black nanny' 'the truth [that] emerges from misrecognition'. In 'Racism and Sexism in Brazilian Culture', Gonzalez writes: 'what we mean to say is that [the black nanny] is not that extraordinary example of total love and dedication that white people make her out to be [...]. She is, quite simply, the mother. That's right, she is the mother. Because the white woman, in fact, is the other.'[2]

The thesis put forward by Rita Segato is the result of eighteen years of reflection on a portrait displayed in the Imperial Museum of Petrópolis in the State Rio de Janeiro—the former summer residence of Portuguese royalty. Rita Segato was visiting the museum when she came across a black nursemaid carrying a white baby in her arms, 'united by an embrace that betrayed an intense amorous seduction'. In the painting, one of the little white hands rested intimately upon the African woman's breast. The scene struck her as excessively familiar, and she recounts that it took her eighteen years to transform that excessive familiarity into a thesis on the colonial Brazilian double motherhood, whose effects extend to our times: the biological white 'civic mother' and the 'transferred' adoptive Black mother. The first, uncensored; the second, forbidden—including in historical and museological discourses, in 'anthropological listening', in the intimate family sphere, and on the psychoanalytic couch.

Hence, the argument published by Rita Segato also announced the following:

In Brazil, motherhoods—from wet nurses to dry nurses; from enslaved Black wet nurses to nannies; from Black domestic workers in general to white mistresses in general—in Brazil, motherhoods are such specific experiences, so specific that it is necessary to take the argument above to its last consequences. According to the Argentine anthropologist, the Brazilian double motherhood—excluded from the canonical records and interpreted away from the complexities of the colonial Oedipus—reverberates in psychoanalytic clinical practice, repeating the 'racialised misogyny' that remains the leitmotif underpinning the Brazilian social scene of the present.

It is necessary to take the argument to its last consequences, as I mentioned, because Brazilian motherhoods have prompted important questions about the maternal function. These are questions that Rita Segato addresses to anthropology—especially kinship studies—and Freudian metapsychology, that is, the primal scene and the Oedipal situation.

I shall give an example of an anthropological (and political) question. Rita Segato tells us about the transition from 'wet' to 'dry'—that is, from obligatory breastfeeding (wet) to other forms of child-rearing (dry). From the enslaved lactating woman to the dry nanny (or 'surrogate mother' or 'foster mother'): why does such a transition take place? We learn from

Rita Segato that the transition from wet to dry was aided by hygienist medical discourse, which was itself concerned with the constitution of a 'slave lineage', biologically determined by the contact between the hungry mouths of white infants and the milky breasts of Black women from Africa. Rita Segato referred to the foundational Brazilian binomial as the 'rosy and carnal baby, clinging in a fusional gesture to the black breast of the one who completes his world, [which] simultaneously projects [...] a public scene and a private scene and, moreover, a publicly private scene.' At the time, around the second half of the nineteenth century, medical discourse epidemiologically associated the wet nurse with the 'transmission of diseases' and with an unavoidable 'moral corruption'. Henceforth, and by medical recommendation, the white child was to suckle exclusively the clean breast of his white biological mother.

Thus was born the nineteenth-century saying, 'one only has one mother'.

All of this because the contact between the white child and the Black wet nurse had come to signify the 'intimacy of the lap', a 'milk bond' that did not coincide with the civilisational diagram of the *casa grande* and *senzala*. In any case, *there* was and still is a biopsychosocial relationship whose 'historical continuity' would culminate in the epidermisation of the Oedipus complex.

But Rita Segato tells us that the beneficiaries of the essential service of human lactation—the white mistresses—were unable to fully uphold either the pathologisation of cross-breastfeeding or the eugenicist prescription that they themselves should nurse their own white offspring. Biomedical governance in the end recommended that white mistresses choose wet nurses from among enslaved women of 'known origin', born and raised within the master's family, as a kind of harm reduction policy. During the global circulation of the novel coronavirus in 2020, some Brazilian states included domestic workers, nannies, and carers for the elderly among 'essential workers'. Essential public services—deemed indispensable for meeting community needs under Brazilian law—include medical and hospital care; the guarding and custody of prisoners; the distribution of electrical energy; funeral services; the use and control of radioactive elements; fire prevention; religious activities; and so on.

I bring another psychoanalytic (and political) question: that of how the enslaved Black mother *is* and *is not* the lost continent for the white heir-child. The Black mother is one continent—among so many—that will possibly come, from wet nurses to dry nurses; from enslaved Black wet nurses to nannies; to Black domestic workers in general. The Black mother is just one of the lost continents among so many others violently annexed. To violently annex the mother—an intimate territory—is to inscribe domination upon the maternal-infant diacritic; a type of inscription that has its consequences, innumerable and explanatory of the so-called 'historical continuity' that maintains the Black domestic worker as a genetic presence in wealthy households which are statistically more white than non-white. Lélia Gonzalez declares: 'she [the black mother] is the mother in the topsy-turvy world of Brazilian culture. As a maid she is the woman; as nanny is the mother. The white woman, the so-called legitimate wife, is precisely the other who, impossible as it may seem, only serves to bear the master's children. She does not perform the maternal function. This is carried out by the Black woman. That is why the "black mother" is the mother.'[3] In the volume prefaced here, when Rita Segato turns to the mothers of the '*povo de santo*', Iemanjá and Oxum, Lélia Gonzalez's quotation marks will be better understood. For my part, I consider the debate surrounding the differential bond attributed to one and the other—both mothers recognised by the mythological key of the African matrix—to be one of the most interesting passages written by Rita Segato for the recognition of Brazilian maternal particularities.

Historically and ethnographically, we Black Brazilian mothers experience scenes of mothering that determine, in a very particular way, the outcome of the fusional encounter between 'the rosy baby' who sucks sustenance from us and 'the black breast'; between the white child-heir and his vector of fulfilment; between coloniality and the sweetened and tamed figure of the esteemed Black woman; between the newborn offspring of the white mistresses—once rosy themselves—and that Black body whose cellular structures were altered by pregnancy, a living appendage circumstantially good for purchase or rent, a nutritional and affective resource advertised in the trade newspapers.

The press of 1850 advertised: 'For sale, a Black woman as a wet nurse, from her first birth and 20 days postpartum.'[4]

It was 2015 when, for the first time postpartum—very much a Black woman in her puerperium—I left my house for an outing. I was to accompany my white sister to the hair salon in an affluent neighbourhood. I was carrying my white son, Antonio, my only child, born some two months earlier. For the first time, he would be taken outside the home and, for the first time, be presented to the predominantly white neighbourhood. My son cried in the hair salon; my sister massaged his little feet and I let a huge, black, hyperpigmented areola spring from my blouse, immediately seized by the white mouth of my white boy. A white woman, adorned with jewellery, addressed my white sister.

'What a beautiful baby. Is he yours?'

The white woman was asking my white sister if the white boy being breastfed by the Black woman belonged to her.

The astonishment at this enactment of the unspoken occupied me for ten years until I could work through it. *Ginecológicas: nascimento negro para além da tragédia* is the name of the book I also wrote, captured by the scene and by a repetition I could not get out of my head; a historical, anthropological, psychic repetition. I had come to understand that this white woman deemed it more legitimate for another white woman to be accompanied by her esteemed Black woman, her wet nurse, in this vivid twenty-first century.[5] A wet nurse was more legitimate in that space reserved for wealthy white women than a Black woman permitted to breastfeed her own child.

The translation of *Black Oedipus* for an Anglophone readership represents the broad circulation of a decisive, carefully constructed thesis on Brazilian social, historical, and psychic formations.

Notes

1 Maria Ribeiro is a social thinker with a Doctorate in Communication and Semiotics (PUC-SP/Université Paris-Diderot). She is a professor on the Postgraduate Programme in Humanities, Rights and Other Legitimacies (PPGHDL/FFLCH) at the University of São Paulo (USP) and on the General Coordination of Specialisation, Advanced Training and Extension (COGEAE) at the Pontifical Catholic University of São Paulo (PUC-SP). She is also Editor-in-Chief of the *International Symposium on Childbirth Assistance* (SIAPARTO), member of the board of the Centre for the Study of Diversities, Intolerance and Conflict (Diversitas/FFLCH-USP), and member of the Peripheral Psychoanalysis Collective. Her postdoctoral research project (FFLCH-USP), entitled *Ginecológicas: o nascimento negro para além da tragédia* (*Gynaecological: Black Birth Beyond Tragedy*), was awarded the non-fiction essay prize by the São Paulo State Programme for Cultural Action (ProAC) and was published in 2023.

2 Lélia Gonzales, 'Racismo e sexism na cultura brasileira', *Ciências Sociais Hoje*, 1 (1981) 223-244. Also available at: https://bibliotecadigital.mdh.gov.br./jspui/handle/192/10316 [last accessed 29 August 2022]. For an English version of the text, see Lélia Gonzalez, 'Racism and Sexism in Brazilian Culture', trans. by Maria Júlia Venâncio, Mateus Mendonça and Gustavo Segat, *New Sociological Perspectives*, vol. 1, no. 1 (2021) 147-159 (p.154).

3 ibid.

4 Clóvis Moura, *Dicionário da Escravidão Negra no Brasil* (São Paulo: Editora da Universidade de São Paulo, 2022) p.30. The foreclosure of the Black child, itself the reason why the milk that feeds the white child is produced in the body of the Black mother, is a matter to which we must return. Clóvis Moura, a Black Brazilian sociologist and historian, tells us that the enslaved child was considered 'an almost dead weight within the values and modes of slave production, since its master had to support it until it became useful as a labour force.' See ibid. p.118.

5 See Maria Ribeiro, *Ginecológicas: nascimento negro para além da tragédia* (São Paulo: Nossa Editora, 2023).

Can One Mother 'Kill' Another?
Preface to the French Edition

Pascale Molinier[1]

Rita Laura Segato's essay, appearing here with her agreement as *Black Oedipus,* was originally published—in Spanish and Portuguese—under the title *The Brazilian Oedipus.* We say 'Black' Oedipus because Brazil is not the only country where white or mixed-race children are handed over to Black nannies: this is common practice in certain Parisian neighbourhoods as well, as recently shown by an ethnographic study carried out by Caroline Ibos.[2] This text therefore does not describe a reality that can be relativised as exotic or distant; it *also* concerns the way some middle-class children are raised—here and now.

To call these nannies 'Black' is not to describe the colour of their skin, though it is generally darker than that of the children they care for, but rather points to the existence of a racialised social relationship that decisively structures the domain of infant care. The Black Oedipus refers to a construction that articulates the political and the psychic within colonial or postcolonial historical configurations. This 'Oedipal' structure only makes sense within its context: the histories of war, conquests, dispossession and impunity; of slavery and, as its consequence, the disdain, passed down over generations, towards the (formerly) colonised and their indigenous cultures. This Oedipus, then, appears clearly as socially and historically situated. It is not an Oedipus of all time or for all time. Nor is it the same in Brazil and in France. This complex is not universal—but is that not always the case? This long-standing debate resurfaces again and again. The fact that human babies are born premature—requiring adults to care for them over an extended period in order to survive and, in turn, become 'grown ups'—is a universal invariant. However, the social organisation of this care has varied considerably across times and societies. *Who does what, how, and with what effectiveness for the child's health and development?* Across time and space, these questions have received strikingly varied and contextual answers.

The Invention of Good Mothers

Maternal love thus seems to be 'an integral part of our familiar world'.[3] 'I couldn't have imagined how much the birth of my son would affect me,' one mother writes. 'It's been the most intense, most indescribable experience of my life. Suddenly, the child we had been hoping for, waiting for, was here. A new human being on Earth—and I am his mother [...] In the end... I can't explain why it's so unsettling... It's inexplicable.'[4]

And yet, 'good mothers'—as well as the emotional subtlety expressed by this particular mother—are a modern invention. The historian Edward Shorter puts it strikingly: 'in traditional societies, mothers were indifferent to the development and happiness of their under-two-year-olds. In modern society, their infant's well-being is the utmost priority.'[5] Until the end of 18th century, many babies, victims of their parents' and nurses' indifference, died while their mothers worked in fields or workshops. They were often left in the care of children barely older than themselves, laid directly on the ground near where their mother laboured, or, in the case of urban families, sent to the countryside, where—if they survived the journey—they were neglected and malnourished by hired caregivers. Eventually, partly under the influence of doctors, mothers began breastfeeding their children themselves to save them from what was referred to as 'the massacre of the innocents'.[6]

Today, mothers read specialised journals and educate themselves about child-rearing. Many still view motherhood as an essential step on the path to a woman's fulfilment. Doctors, pedagogues, paediatricians, psychologists and psychoanalysts have carried the torch of the 'good mother', seen as indispensable not just to the child's survival but also to its proper development. This model prevails in Western societies. Mothers—with a capital M—are seen as the natural providers of primary care. It is always seen as preferable if it is the Mother who breastfeeds, plays with the child, gives them a bath or accompanies them on school outings. *The Mother is irreplaceable*—and yet she is often replaced. A mother who wishes to step away thus feels burdened with the delicate task of supervising, as carefully as possible, the delegation of childcare: of selecting the best person or institution to perform a function understood as supplementary or substitutive.

'We are starting to question *not the mother's essential role,*' the psychoanalyst Gisèle Harrus-Révidi pointedly writes, '*but her obligatory and guilt-ridden subjugation to the child* and, by consequence, her relationship to her work. Finally, what we often see in clinical work is that fulfilled mothers who have delegated secondary care to others enable their child—who may, of course, have been deprived of tenderness in early childhood—to flourish later on, through identification, just like their mother.'[7] This sentence, which concludes her preface to a translation of D.W. Winnicott—the apostle of the 'good-enough mother'—thus argues for a 'conciliation' between the legitimate interests of mothers and those of their children. This conciliation is made possible by the presence of 'others'—here left undefined—who carry out what she calls 'secondary' caregiving tasks.

This brings us to the heart of the matter: the subordination of certain people to the Mother. Today in France, this subordination falls to globalised nannies who have chosen to migrate to the former colonial power because they speak its language. 'The relationship between the two women', Ibos writes, 'is a political relationship, substantially asymmetrical, both at its origin and in the way it unfolds. Employers do not know—or pretend not to know—that hiring a nanny means bringing politics into the living room.'[8] I would add, drawing on Segato's perspective, that it also means introducing politics into the child's psyche. And this is, no doubt, the most unsettling aspect of her incisive essay.

Mothers 'Blown Away by the Wind'

Women work to survive and/or flourish—and this is nothing new. Simply put, mothers often have other things to do besides looking after their children full-time, and they partially delegate this care work to other people, preferably other women. There are the staff of crèches, childminders who provide childcare in their own homes, and nannies [*nounous*] who work in their employer's homes—the new proletarians of globalisation. Migrant women from poorer countries offer a service that Western employers tend to define not in terms of actual skills or training but through essentialised emotional qualities associated with a particular race or ethnicity. Employers are generally content to simply acknowledge in nannies just enough 'human warmth' to avoid having to pay them properly. Their exotic origins other them just enough to also ensure that the Mother is not truly *replaced* by this subaltern stand-in, who is, in effect, chosen from a catalogue of stereotypes. In France, when it comes to small children, African women are in high demand, while Asian women are perceived as 'cold' and North Africans as 'harsh with children' (plus, they observe Ramadan and some wear a headscarf): 'A friend told me that when her daughter was crying because she didn't want to nap, the nanny would hold her against her chest and rock her to sleep while singing lullabies. I really like these customs, the way they are with children. So, I guess I would *a priori* prefer an African woman over an Asian or North African one.'[9]

Systemic racism is key to understanding how economically active women—university-educated and seeing themselves as progressive—are able to entrust their little angels to another woman they consider 'loving', without too much guilt, and then dismiss her without hesitation when she is no longer useful.[10] Nannies have a very short lifespan. Because they perform what is considered 'secondary' care from a naturalised and devalued position, they are often tossed aside like Kleenex at the start of the holiday season, disappearing from sight and eventually from memory once the child enters nursery—replaced by young au-pairs (to support language learning and boost a future CV) or by 'play-based learning activities' outside the home. From the very beginning of the relationship, all the justifications are already in place to legitimise this planned, inevitable 'disappearance'.

Here, too, the catalogue of stereotypes—negative ones this time—proves to be a useful ally. The 'customary' qualities so desirable for rearing *infants* must be reconsidered in light of an imagined carelessness, uncleanliness, and fondness for anything that sparkles. 'Africans are brilliant with kids; they get attached to children like Scarlett O'Hara's nanny in *Gone with the Wind.* A dream nanny! But okay, alongside that, they have a reputation for doing nothing, spending their time at Sunlight looking for trinkets, and being sloppy with the ironing.'[11]

Here we see that the nanny is not only asked to care for the children, but—for the same price—also to perform domestic chores. What a shame it can't last. This flow of maternal affect is not swept away by the wind but by the market-driven movement of 'emotional capitalism'.[12]

This enables the Mother to preserve her unique and irreplicable place in the child's heart. The memories of the nanny—she hopes, more or less consciously—will be erased thanks to the providential mechanism of infantile amnesia. Living up to the modern demands of being a 'good-enough' mother requires a double sacrifice. Not only that of the nanny's own children who, left behind, have permanently lost their mother—but also that of the white children of working mothers, who once slept peacefully on the African breast, lulled by lullabies. That, too, is over.

And yet, in a dramatic turn of events, Segato's essay contests and throws into crisis the very notion of care as 'secondary' or 'supplementary' simply because it is provided by 'secondary' persons—women 'blown away by the wind'. However, child development specialists say it clearly: nothing matters more than early attachments. A child without care does not exist, as Winnicott puts it. 'Everything counts in the relationship: the way of holding the child, of handling him, of living together', including the way the father is included.[13] For Winnicott, *holding* depends on a three-dimensional relationship: one's own body, the mother, and time. *And who is this mother?* She is the person who provides care and a secure environment, as Harrus-Révidi writes. Segato takes psychoanalysis at its word. She denaturalises motherhood by disentangling the biological and legal mothers—the mother who gives birth, or in the case of adoption is officially designated in the civil registry, from the mother who provides primary care.

In the ideology of the 'good mother'—which includes even the more realistic 'good-enough mother'—these two mothers are collapsed into one. *They must become one.* It is the duty of the biological and legal mother to provide primary care to her child. And if she does not? Punishment follows in the form of cutting or sneering comments from her own mother, her sisters or friends, her father or the child's father, her boss or work colleagues. It can even affect her professionally: how can you trust a woman who neglects her children? If a woman does not feel this guilt and drops her kid at the crèche with ease, she is seen as highly suspect and would do better to feign heartbreak at having to *abandon* her child. External criticism may be irritating, but it is no doubt easier to reject and rationalise than the guilt that constantly threatens mothers from within. The norms of motherhood are so deeply internalised that women who become mothers must constantly, and painfully, confront the gap between the ideal 'good mother' and the mother they actually are—not even 'good enough'.[14]

The maternal position—in a society that is tyrannical towards mothers—is thus grounded in a *psychosocial* guilt, one that is perfectly contingent in the sense that it has no roots in psycho-infantile history but rather in the untenable place of mothers within the gender system. As Harrus-Révidi rightly points out, this place requires that mothers be subjugated to their children. Inverting the ideal, to become a mother is to become a servant. His Majesty the Baby is, of course, completely dependent on others, but in the 'good mother' system his dependence becomes his mother's enslavement. Nothing remains the same in a couple after the birth of a first child. If only it were just a matter of taking care of him! But the entire sphere of domestic work becomes the feminine domain par excellence. Among the middle classes, nannies and other domestic workers take on chores that resist the division of domestic labour, all in the service of conjugal peace.[15]

Segato performs a feminist act by dismantling the unified and natural image of the Mother, while simultaneously critiquing the subalternity of the Nanny and its erasure. Yes, the reader has understood correctly: Segato dares to call 'mothers' these women who are paid to perform a maternal function—a function that, contrary to what guilt-ridden mothers would like to believe, is not secondary or supplementary but primary or even primordial, at least from the child's point of view. In the Black Oedipus, the archaic or pre-Oedipal mother is not (or not always) the Mother.

Bonaparte's Double Oedipus

Psychoanalysis has largely contributed to women's subjugation to the role of the mother—the desire for a child often taken as proof that a woman has fulfilled her femininity—and to the normative unification of the maternal function in the figure of the biological and/or legal mother. Yet Freud was particularly interested in the specific role of nannies, whom he viewed with considerable suspicion, especially because of their 'old nannies' tales', stories that, along with the wolf and the bogeyman, conveyed menacing messages of castration.[16] Freud's ambivalent interest, as well as its limits, is perhaps most strikingly revealed in the reflections of Princess Marie Bonaparte on her own psychoanalysis.[17]

Once upon a time, there was a little princess whose mother died of an embolism just one month after giving birth, and who was therefore raised by nannies. Forty-two years later, after her father's death, Marie Bonaparte found among his papers five diaries she had written between the ages of seven and a half and ten. 'I read them', she wrote, 'and had the strange impression that, even though I had written them, I had no recollection of them.' The enigma of this experience—as well as the supposedly grotesque nature of the diaries themselves—was one of the reasons, 'among others', that led her to seek analysis with Freud.

As usual, Freud didn't beat around the bush. When Bonaparte recounted a dream in which she was lying in a lower bed than the one she was observing, looking up 'at a household she knew, lying in a large adult bed', he 'asserted' that she must have witnessed sexual scenes in broad daylight during her early childhood. 'I protested', Bonaparte writes, 'I had never had a mother! But Freud replied that I did have a nanny.'[18]

Having resisted Freud's interpretation and finding it absurd, Bonaparte embarked on a genuine detective-style investigation into her childhood. She asked Pascal—her father's Corsican groom, who was also his illegitimate half-brother and bore a striking resemblance to him—about the primal scene. Household rumours had long suggested that this 'uncle' had had an affair with little Marie's nanny. The elderly man confirmed that he, in fact, used to come up to the nursery every day to check on the child, supposedly fulfilling a promise he had made to Marie's mother on her deathbed. Pressed by the headstrong princess, he eventually admitted that his visits had a more carnal motivation: his affair with the nanny had lasted from the time the princess was six months old until she was three and a half. It was also the reason her grandmother had ultimately dismissed the nanny.

Silent in her crib, the princess had seen everything! Her writing at the age of seven bore a distorted trace of this experience: a pencil in her mouth, referring to fellatio. Freud had not been wrong; the groom had confirmed everything. Bonaparte writes: 'as a child, I went through at least two Oedipus complexes in succession: the first in which the Oedipal couple was Pascal and the Nanny; the second still involved my father, but first married to my mother—"Little Mummy", as I was told to call her—and then my father "remarried" to his own mother, my grandmother, "Good Mummy", as I came to know her. These Oedipus complexes, projected one onto the other, no doubt often made it difficult to untangle what was primal from what had been added on.'[19] Relationships with servants were integrated into Bonaparte's double Oedipus; however, contrary to the Brazilian Oedipus described by Segato, the entangled situations revolve around a classical triangulation in which the heterosexual relationship between adults—the famous primal scene—remains central.

What Bonaparte identifies as the success of her analysis is a brilliant exercise in unveiling archaic, repressed material. Everything seems miraculously illuminated, like a well-constructed detective novel. Everything? Not quite—a strange resistance remains, located in a recurring childhood nightmare, organised around a single signifier: *the Serquintué*—a made-up word naming a train that bursts into her childhood bedroom, killing everything it *sees,* while the dreamer never manages to fully hide. And yet the dream of the Serquintué escapes Freud's usually sharp perception.

He reads it merely as a confirmation of his own theories: a reversal of active into passive—not having to see in reality, not being seen in the dream. But neither Freud nor his analysand were satisfied with this interpretation. It was only after the analysis had ended, in a car taking her away from Freud, that Marie Bonaparte 'suddenly grasped the enigma' of Serquintué.[20] She was finally able to unravel the knot of signifiers: *Serg* (from *Sarg,* German for 'coffin'), *tué* ('killed') and *quin,* as in *requin* ('shark'), designating her grandmother, who, according to the household gossip, had rejoiced at Little Mummy's death, which enabled her to seize control of the inheritance and even, for the same reasons, was said to have poisoned her, in collusion with her son. The *Serquintué* thus condenses the hearse bearing the mother—killed by the sexual act—which returns as a train, panting and charging 'like a furious bull', to kill the little girl who, not content with having killed her mother by being born, also watched the spectacle of the sexual act with pleasure. Bonaparte concludes: 'Pascal's partner, Nanny, had also "died" of it, in her own way. Didn't my grandmother send her *away* when I was three years old? But from a child's perspective, as well as for the unconscious, going away for good equals *dying*.'[21]

Even though it is not racialised, the configuration described by Bonaparte seems to me closely related to that of the Black Oedipus, in terms of the deeply tragic tonality of the 'two mothers' *lost*—both sacrificed to satisfy the grandmother-shark who wished for or caused their death.[22] In the Brazilian configuration, as Segato notes, it is dominant women—mothers, grandmothers—rather than men who intervene as the third party to separate the *infans* from his *madre-negra*. For her part, Bonaparte shows how traumatic this separation can be: 'from a child's perspective, as well as for the unconscious,' as she so aptly puts it, 'going away for good equals *dying*.'[23] Moreover, the nanny is not only 'dead': she's erased, without trace, without grave—'foreclosed'.

Foreclosure is a term that appears frequently in Segato's work.[24] She uses it in a sense closer to Judith Butler than to Jacques Lacan, to designate what is socially barred from consciousness, what remains unsaid, unwritten, unmarked or untranslated within a history that is both collective and individual. In this case, it is the mother of primary care, the Black, mixed-race or Indigenous mother, who is foreclosed, i.e., not inscribed in the Symbolic. It is in her arms, her voice, her scent that the child nonetheless began to form its psyche and its erotic body, its body of drives. She's the seductress, as brilliantly shown by the colonial painting analysed by Segato, which appears within this book. But she is not pure sensuality: she is also an educator and a speaking subject. To believe that the nanny would stick to the strict register of *lullabies*—as the hip Parisian mother put it—is a (post-)colonial fantasy.

The cultural breadth of what falls under this foreclosure is powerfully described by another psychoanalyst, Maud Mannoni, in her reflections on her own Sinhala nanny, who cared for her until the age of six and whom she lost when her parents left Java to return to Europe. Between her Aya and the Hindi porter, little Maud's life was woven into the country's legends, which taught her to speak to snakes and crows, and not to harm them. All these fantastic stories were told to her in Hindi. 'Then came the event that disrupted my universe,' she writes, 'a separation from Aya, which I experienced as an abandonment all the more terrifying because not a word was said about it. In my distress, I could no longer tell *who I was,* or *where I was going.* I didn't know what was happening to me.'[25] Within three months, she lost her command of English and 'incidentally, Hindi', her two mother tongues. 'I lost my ability to speak,' she writes. In this case, it was Aya who refused to follow the family to Europe. Like the 'real' mother, nannies are also not entirely subject to the child's desire.

Speaking about her family life, Mannoni later wrote: 'A nanny was looking after our son, much to Octave's [her husband's] dismay—he had dreamt of a mother who would be available twenty-four-seven. But I was only able to be a mother with the help of a *substitute mother* [*mère d'appoint*], and the safety of an environment in which each person could have the peace and privacy they needed.'[26] This modest position—which recognises *one's own need* for a 'substitute mother', a caregiving system that implies two mothers—is unusual, even if we admit that 'substitute' is no less inadequate a term than 'secondary'. It is surely no coincidence that this gesture of dis-idealisation of motherhood comes from a woman who chose, for the cover of her autobiography *What Truth Lacks in Order to be Said,* a photograph of herself under the age of two, held in the arms of her Black nanny. What truth lacks in order to be said, Mannoni writes, are mute inscriptions or 'impressions', like the lost history of which the photograph captures a trace. Family history, or the family romance, according to her, always 'appears as a *semblant,* with a gap between the killed truth and what has been left as knowledge in individual memory.'[27] This gap, she writes, returns in what belongs—like a fragment of truth—to the register of the unanalysable.

As we have seen, the murder of the mother of infant care represented a point of resistance in the princess' analysis with Freud. The Black Oedipus is founded on the existence of power relationships between women competing for the place of the Mother. From among several rivalling mothers, only one is left standing. In Bonaparte's history, the nanny is a peasant girl, and 'Little Mummy'—her biological mother—is much younger than 'Good Mummy', the grandmother, who ultimately exerts power over the other women. The fact remains that the princess could not be the daughter of a peasant, and her separation from her nanny—now foreclosed—inscribes the little girl *in a social order structured by class rather than by gender.* That same hierarchical social order, as theorised by Segato, weaves together class and race in a common framework. We can see that, in order to live in Europe, Mannoni had to shed her colonial attributes, to no longer speak Hindi; her separation from Aya was part of her whitening.[28]

Whiteness and the Rupture of Early Attachments

For Freud, the Oedipus complex was a differentiator between generations and sexes, governed by the primacy of the phallus. In the Black Oedipus, the differentiating force at work is instead social and racial, marking—for some children of the privileged classes—one's entry into whiteness. Studies of whiteness have examined 'the ways in which certain social groups come to be seen as "white" and, in the former colonial empires, come to occupy a hegemonic position in the context of racist ideology that associates white skin with purity, neutrality or universality.'[29] Like France and other countries, Brazil is a former colonial empire. We must study not just the racialised but also the ones who *racialise* and the dynamics involved in the production of 'white identities'—or, as Maxime Cervulle points out, citing Toni Morrison, ask 'what racism does to those who perpetuate it'.[30]

This work has typically been carried out—following in the footsteps of Frantz Fanon and Colette Guillaumin—with regards to adults. Segato, by contrast, interrogates the construction of whiteness in very young children. In a colonial-style political system or its postcolonial remnants, 'those responsible for the child's care'—the mothers who provide primary care—are devalued and naturalised as Black, in order to secure the victory of the Mother. What is foreclosed here is not the mother's desire for the father; what most decisively introduces a third term is her desire—or need—to work, to love her work more than, or just as much as, her child.

This highlights one of the limits of what feminism has not yet managed to fully deconstruct: the modern illusion underpinning motherhood as the tyrannical feminine ideal. This is not to deny the importance of parenthood as an experience—for both men and women—and still less so to reject it, à la Simone de Beauvoir. Rather, it is a matter of restoring this experience to its rightful place in women's lives; it cannot be the whole of it.

A Racial Melancholia?

Segato's anthropological work focuses on the analysis of violence—and more specifically, femicide, the lethal violence against women.[31] In one of her key works, *The Elementary Structures of Violence,* she adopts a perspective she defines as transcultural, through which she interprets the Freudo-Lacanian Oedipal narrative as a modern myth that 'culturalises'—through the narratives specific to the Western nuclear family—the *primal scene,* schema or structure, of what we call the symbolic. That is, a structure of relations between certain positions: *the maternal* (whoever embodies it), *the filial,* fused in an Edenic state which only gains autonomy, and the rules of social life through the intervention—always brutal—of a male legislative agent, *the paternal.*

This schema appears in many myths that institute hierarchy, and is repeated in racial, colonial or gender relationships. The universal, Segato writes, is not Oedipus, but 'the unequal structure of patriarchy'. Yet, unlike the myths of traditional societies—Segato mainly draws on Maurice Godelier's work on the Baruya—the Freudo-Lacanian myth, she claims, is deceptive.[32] It fools us by keeping silent about the foundational violence at the heart of patriarchy and its endless repetition in order to reproduce the Law (of the Father). Can other myths, other narratives, be created? What would it mean to exhume the figure of the nanny?

What remains unsaid and unwritten in the stories of contemporary white babies, cradled by Black mothers who were swept away by the wind, is precisely the colonial structure that governs the relationship between their two mothers. The matrix of whiteness is based on the repudiation (orchestrated by the legal mother) of the mother who provided infant care. In a single gesture of rupture and effacement, the construction of whiteness demands that the carnal, but also the cultural, bond with the Black mother be forgotten; that the incorporation of hybridity be denied, in order to solidify the binaries of *us versus them* that underlie racist ideology.

If whiteness is acquired through the repudiation of an early attachment to a non-white woman, can we say that this figure is both lost and, simultaneously, internalised melancholically? Could one speak, paraphrasing Butler's gender melancholia, of a racial melancholia?[33]

We find another story of origin in Frida Kahlo's 1937 painting *My Nurse and I.* She depicts herself with an adult face and a child's body, wearing a night dress, cradled in the arms of her Indigenous nanny, her lips slightly parted beneath the woman's breast. The nurse is naked to her waist; her skin is much darker than Frida's. Still, the artist does not portray herself as a white child but as a dark-skinned *métisse*, with very dark hair and a faint moustache above her lips—a trace of her European heritage. The nanny wears an Olmec mask, drawn from Mexico's oldest and most mysterious pre-Columbian culture.[34] She is large, her face hidden, placing her entirely on the side of the archaic. In the background, we see a lush natural landscape evoking a kind of original Paradise. However, the sense of abundance and wholeness is contradicted. The milk flowing from the nurse's breast is rendered as raindrops falling from a dark sky, like tears. The entire image conveys the dramatic intensity of a fragment of truth; the nurse is terrifying rather than seductive—or perhaps terrified under her mask—we do not know. What the colonial painting—a white and masculine vision—depicts as seduction, Kahlo—her hybrid and feminine gaze—casts in the light of a melancholic disaffection. This 'unanalysable' inscription confronts us as uncanny, as strange. This is also the power of Segato's essay: challenging essentialist notions of identity, giving voice to subjects and attachments foreclosed by modern myths, and rendering white people—most often presumed self-evident—strangers to themselves.

Translated from the French by
Kristina Valendinova,
London, July, 2025

Notes

1 Pascale Molinier is Professor of Psychology at the University of Paris 13, Villetaneuse. She is the author of, among other works, *Qu'est-ce que le care? Souci des autres, sensibilité, responsabilité* (with Sandra Laugier and Patricia Paperman) (Paris: Payot, 2009). This preface was originally published in French in Rita Segato, *L'œdipe Noir: Des nourriceset des mères* (Paris: Payot, 2022).

Acknowledgements:

I would like to thank Mara Viveros Vigolla, who introduced me to Rita Segato's work, and to thank Lise Gaignard for our many feminist discussions of motherhood.

- Pascale Molinier

2 I draw extensively on Ibos' remarkable work, which has informed much of what follows. See Caroline Ibos, *Qui gardera nos enfants? Les nounous et les mères* (Paris: Flammarion, 2012).

3 See Edward Shorter, *The Making of the Modern Family* (New York: Harper Collins, 1976).

4 Ibos, op cit. p.20.

5 Shorter, op cit . p.209

6 ibid.

7 Gisèle Harrus-Révidi, 'Soins et amour maternel' [2011], preface to Donald W. Winnicott, *La Relation parent-nourissons,* trans. by Jeanine Kalmanovitch (Paris: Payot, 2011) p. 26 (my emphasis).

8 Ibos, op cit. p.14.

9 ibid. p.42.

10 Systemic racism—acted without thought or reflection—is the interface between 'interactional and structural forms of racism. The former are constituted by repetitive and corrosive "micro-inequalities", while the latter by procedural rules governing how individuals are treated. Both forms are embedded in the ordinary functioning [...] of the entire society'. (See Véronique de Rudder and François Vourc'h, 'Les discriminations racistes dans le monde du travail', in *De la question sociale à la question raciale? Représenter la société française,* ed. by Didier Fassin and Éric Fassin (Paris: La Découverte, 2006) p.179.)

11 Ibos, op cit. p.43.

12 See Arlie R. Hochschild, 'Ethique du care et capitalism', in *Contre l'indifférence des privilegiés. À quoi sert le care*, ed. by Patricia Paperman and Pascale Molinier (Paris : Payot, 2013) pp.69-97.

13 Harrus-Révidi, op cit. p.22.

14 Winnicott's term, meant to relieve maternal guilt, is still largely misleading, because even 'good-enough' is already a lot.

15 See Pascale Molinier, 'Des féministes et leurs femmes de ménage: entre réciprocité du care et souhait de dépersonnalisation', *Multitudes*, 37-38 (2009) 113-121.

16 'Usually it is from women that the threat emanates; very often they seek to strengthen their authority by a reference to the father or the doctor, who, so they say, will carry out the punishment.' And later: 'we should not be as short-sighted as the person in charge of the child.' See Sigmund Freud, 'The Dissolution of the Oedipus Complex' (1924), trans. by Joan Riviere, in *The Standard Edition of the Complete Psychological Works of Sigmund Freud, Volume XIX (1923-1925):* The Ego and the Id *and Other Works*, ed. by James Strachey, with Anna Freud, assisted by Alix Strachey and Alan Tyson, 24 vols (London: Vintage, 2001) XIX, p.174 and p.176.

17 Marie Bonaparte, *Cinq cahiers écrits par une petite fille entre sept ans et demi et dix ans. Et leur commentaires* (Paris: Imprimé pour l'auteur, 1939). Extracts from the first notebook, p.3 and p.6, and pp.58-78, were published in *L'Infini,* 2 (1983) 76-89.

18 ibid. p.68.

19 ibid. p.80.

20 ibid. p.85.

21 ibid. p.87.

22 Even though the princess describes the Corsican peasants who serve her as 'primitives', Pascal is 'devoted, like the savages, to their clan'. See ibid. p.81.

23 ibid. p.87.

24 See, for example, Rita Segato, *Las Estructuras elementales de la violencia. Ensayos sobre género entre la antropología, el psicoanálisis y los derechos humanos* (Buenos Aires: Universidad Nacional de Quilmes/Prometeo, 2003).

25 Maud Mannoni, *Ce qui manque à la vérité pour être dite* (Paris: Denoël, 1988) p.16.

26 ibid, p.31 (my emphasis).

27 ibid, p.77 and p.78.

28 Mannoni writes that Françoise Dolto thought that her own biological mother was more or less an idiot, which Mannoni does not quite deny: highlighting her relationship with Aya is also a re-creation of a more suitable filiation, the daughter's revenge against mothers, including Dolto.

29 Maxime Cervulle, *Dans le blanc des yeux. Diversité, racisme et médias* (Paris: Éditions Amsterdam, 2013).

30 ibid. p.19.

31 See Rita Segato, *La Escritura en el cuerpo de las mujeres asesinadas en Ciudad Juárez. Territorio, soberanía y crímenes de segundo estado* (Mexico: Universidad del Claustro de Sor Juana, 2006).

32 See Maurice Godelier, *La Production des Grands hommes. Pouvoir et domination masculine chez les Baruya de Nouvelle-Guinée* (Paris: Fayard, 1982).

33 For Judith Butler, heterosexuality, another hegemonic position, this time in the hierarchical order of sexualities, is in fact based on a gender melancholia. According to them, 'gender is acquired at least in part through the repudiation of homosexual attachments; the girl becomes a girl through being subject to a prohibition which bars the mother as an object of desire and installs that barred object as a part of the ego, indeed, as a melancholic identification. Thus the identification contains within it both the prohibition and the desire, and so embodies the ungrieved loss of the homosexual cathexis. If one is a girl to the extent that one does not want a girl, then wanting a girl will bring being a girl into question; within this matrix, homosexual desire thus panics gender.' Judith Butler, *The Psychic Life of Power: Theories of Subjection* (Stanford, CA: Stanford University Press, 1997) p.136. According to Butler, the heterosexual man desires the woman he would never want to be. His desire will be haunted by the panic of becoming what he desires.

34 See also what Segato later says about La Malinche in *Black Oedipus*.

Black Oedipus

Coloniality and the Foreclosure of Gender and Race[1]

Rita Segato

For Marcosidé Valdivia,
the Black housekeeper
who nursed my mother in Uruburu,
La Pampa, Argentina, in 1913

Forms of Fatherhood in Classical Ethnography

One of the most fascinating chapters in the history of anthropology begins with Bronisław Malinowski's analysis, undertaken in the 1920s, of the forms of paternity found in the Trobriand Islands (including Kiriwina) in the Melanesian archipelago in the Western Pacific. In the Trobriand Islanders' avuncular, matrilineal, and patrilocal society, two positions are sharply distinguished from one another: the *kagadu,* or mother's brother, from whom children inherit land, a name, and the claims of belonging to a village and clan, and the *tama,* or mother's husband, who is a playmate, a beloved figure, and an object of filial attachment in everyday life. While the *kagadu* embodies patriarchal authority, the *tama* lavishes paternal affection on the child.

> A father, in all discussions about relationship, was pointedly described to me by the natives as *Tomakava,* a "stranger," or even more correctly, an "outsider." This expression would also be frequently used in conversation when the natives argued about some point of inheritance, or tried to justify some line of behavior, or when in a quarrel the position of the father was to be belittled. I have used the word "father" so far to indicate the relationship as found in the society of the Trobriand Islanders, but it must have been clear to the reader that this word must be taken, not with the various legal, moral, and biological implications that it has for us, but in a sense entirely specific to the society with which we are dealing. It would have been best, in order to avoid introducing a real misconception, not to have used our word "father," but the native one *tama,* and to have spoken of the "*tama* relationship" instead of "fatherhood."[2]

In the Trobriand Islands, because of the prevalence of a matrilineal principle of genealogy, lines of descent run through the mother, and *patria potestas* or parental authority is held by the maternal uncle;

meanwhile places of residence are determined by a principle of patrilocality, meaning that the child and mother live in the father's village. After the discovery of systems of kinship like this one—in which the figure of the father is doubled—anthropology came to address and debate the difference, already extant in Roman law, between the *pater* and the *genitor*. In fact, we should distinguish between three different types of paternity: that of the *pater* or juridical father; that of the mother's husband; and that of the *genitor* or biological father, who is in fact not necessarily the mother's husband.[3]

Anthropologists devoted beautiful and extensive pages to the problems that followed from this initial discovery. These were problems related to the universality of the Oedipus complex and ignorance of biological paternity, that is, of the male's role in the conception of the child, repeatedly underscored by the 'natives' discussed in Malinowski's notes on his extensive fieldwork. The Trobriand Islanders' theory of human reproduction, at least during the period when Malinowski conducted research among them, suggests that the spirit of an ancestor returns and is embodied in the uterus of a pregnant woman; the semen of her partner is not considered relevant to this process. Reflecting on his discoveries, Malinowski himself asked about the universality of the Oedipus complex. In my view, his argument anticipated contemporary understandings of the doubling of the Oedipal structure and its concrete manifestations in the Trobriand Islanders' society:

he argued that in this context the Oedipal triangle involved not the child's biological father but a figure from its mother's familial universe: her brother. The psychoanalyst Ernest Jones took this as a negation of Freud's theory, and this gave rise to what became known as the debate between Jones and Malinowski.[4] This debate continued after Malinowski's death, in the work of the anthropologist Melford Spiro, who took issue with Malinowski's reading of the manifestations of the Oedipus complex among the Trobriand Islanders. Spiro argued against Edmund Leach, and in particular against what Leach considered to be a belief in 'virgin birth,' an understanding of conception that left out the intervention of the mother's husband. According to Spiro, there could not be Oedipal conflict with a maternal uncle, because this figure does not have sexual access to the child's mother, and Oedipal conflict results from the father's sexual monopoly on the mother, rather than from a challenge to paternal authority. The fact that the father or *tama* does not exercise power or authority over the child and, on the contrary, that he is the child's affectionate playmate, for Spiro, makes the Oedipus complex much more severe and dramatic for the Trobriand Islanders than it is in the West, in the sense that the child of Trobriand Islanders finds himself completely unable to register or leave any trace of his antagonistic relation to his father, who is in this context a friend who does not wield power over the child. This was shown, Spiro argued, by the total absence of paternal figures in dreams and myths, an absence that proved the immense difficulty of symbolizing antagonism in the Trobriand Islanders' society. Repression here took extreme forms, and all possible ways of processing Oedipal ambivalence were blocked.[5]

The debate between Leach and Spiro about Trobriand Islanders' ignorance of the father's biological role in the reproductive process remains in conversation with Malinowski's work. Leach launched this debate by refusing the literal interpretation of Malinowski's finding that the Trobriand Islanders were 'ignorant' of biological paternity. For Leach, this 'ignorance' was an expression of social organization. In other words, the Trobriand Islanders' stated ignorance or 'non-knowledge' about biological reproduction was in fact a metaphorical knowledge of the field of social reproduction and the workings of lineage. The natives' statements of their ignorance of the father's role in conception were, for Leach, social statements and not the statements about biology that they at first appeared to be.[6]

Initially, Spiro intervenes in this debate by accepting Malinowski's claims about the Trobriand Islanders' 'ignorance' of biological paternity, that is, their absence of scientific knowledge on the subject. Later, however, he adopts another approach, arguing, as in his interpretation of the Oedipus complex in the Trobriands, that here 'ignorance' should be understood as a form of repression.[7]

> Ignorance, however, may result not only from the absence of knowledge concerning some fact or event, but also from its banishment from conscious awareness; to employ the technical term, it may result from *denial*. [T]he adoption of this meaning of 'ignorance' would suggest that although the Trobrianders are cognizant of the reproductive role of the father, they disavow this knowledge because it is threatening or painful.[8]

Thus whereas Leach reads 'ignorance' as a statement about society, Spiro reads it as a statement about the psyche.

Brazilian Mothers in the Historical and Statistical Record

I have presented a very succinct account of these sophisticated and sustained anthropological debates in order to shed light on a lacuna in Brazilian anthropology's reflections on the structures of kinship.[9] I am referring to a phenomenon that is omnipresent in Brazil, but on the mother's side: a splitting or doubling of the maternal function that involves a biological mother and a juridical one, or a mother and a 'de facto' mother who does not count, or a mother proper and a nurse or nanny.[10] Here during the colonial period and after it, until the second half of the nineteenth century, 'historically enduring practices' included the use of wetnurses to provide what Suely Gomes Costa has called 'transferred motherhood.' These wetnurses were 'already present in social life during the earliest days of the colonial period'; then beginning in the nineteenth century their roles were reduced until they became dry nurses or 'nannies,' or *babás* in Portuguese.[11] These figures are still omnipresent in bourgeois Brazilian homes. The lacuna, gap, or blindness in Brazilian ethnography and historiography thus leads us to confront a question that will not be silent. It is a question about silence precisely. And silence is precisely what this essay seeks to investigate.

> It fell to enslaved black women to act as wetnurses. This led to the creation of the figure of the black mother, a figure so clearly present in Brazilian literature. [...] The use of wetnurses, initially a practice among upper-class families, became more common also among members of the urban middle class beginning in the nineteenth century. This can be proven by the remarkable frequency of announcements in the press either offering or seeking the services of wetnurses for hire; it can also be shown by the constant presence of the question of wetnursing in medical discourse during this period.[12]

The displacement of the wetnurse by the dry nurse as substitute mother was a consequence of the hygienic pressures brought to bear on society by doctors and in the press during this period: 'Because she nurtured the newborn from the first precarious moments of its life, the person of the wet-nurse became for the patrões [employers, or masters] the most terrible and alarming carrier of diseases'.[13] However, documents attest to the fact that families who employed wetnurses during this period did not submit to the demands of medical modernity and forgo these women's services. This tension led to the formation of compromises whereby families both employed wetnurses and took precautions related to their backgrounds and health, especially in urban contexts.

> Despite advice to patrões as late as 1893 that they should choose as wet-nurses 'women whose origins and life are well known, raised by the family, for example,' urban conditions did not permit such close scrutiny. ... [M]ost relied on locally hired women, either slave or free.[14]

This same period also saw the emergence of abolitionist critiques, motivated by various projects. I am thinking, for instance, of figures like the writer Joaquim Manuel de Macedo, author of the novel *As vítimas-algozes* (The Victim-Executioners, 1869), figures who called for an end to slavery not for humanitarian reasons but to protect whites from the contamination and moral corruption that blacks supposedly introduced into the intimate space of the seignorial home.[15] The virulence of these critiques is striking. The most violent critiques of the period target the humble providers of maternal services, who lend their affection and offer care to the children of white and whitened families. These critiques are shot through with intense hatred; they were surely written by men who in their own infancy had been lulled to sleep at the breasts of women just like these. These expressions of hate contrast with the notes of appreciation addressed to clean white mothers, wealthy mothers, with their commendable breasts. The well-known phrase that recurs in the discourse of Latin American hygienists—'there is only one mother'—can be traced to this period as well.

However, it is clear that the state did not arrive at a public solution to the problem of childcare—whether for white or black children—in the form of nurseries.[16] Nor did the families—not all of them wealthy—with access to the means to hire nannies agree to give up this privilege. But what did take place was the transformation of wetnurses into dry nurses.

Few academic studies touch on the ambivalence of the wetnurse during the late colonial or slave periods or this figure's direct condemnation by the authorised voices within Brazilian society.[17] The practice of 'transferred motherhood' and the kinds of relations that it surely generated, both for those who enjoyed the privilege of hiring wetnurses and for those who provided the service for 500 uninterrupted years, have left a trace in Brazilian literature. But they are absent in analyses of and reflections on Brazil's history. The scant attention paid to the figure of the wetnurse in the scholarly literature written in Brazil contrasts with the vast reach and the historical centrality of the practice as well as its forceful impact on the national psyche.

This *absence or missing inscription* within academic writing is also a point of departure for this essay. Here my aim is not to engage in a torturous use and abuse of a textual body; I do not seek to extract a *relation* from this body with figurative forceps. I am not dealing, in other words, with a relation of the kind found in the saga written by Gilberto Freyre, whose work is marked by an emphasis on *customs* that have now found their way into law (as in Article 5(a) of the Convention on the Elimination of all forms of Discrimination Against Women). Rather, on the contrary, I understand the wetnurse's *absence* here as an idiosyncratic form of foreclosure, a foreclosure of the name-of-the-mother. My reading is in keeping with what Judith Butler argues in their elaborations on the Lacanian concept of foreclosure, as I will show below. This foreclosure of the name-of-the-mother could also be described in a more orthodox way—that is, a way more in keeping with Lacan's interpretation of psychosis as a (psychotic) foreclosure of the name of the father—although it points to a specific shortcoming of the paternal metaphor: its inability to name and grammaticalise the mother.

It is, as always, through statistics that we can trace the contemporary persistence of the black mother as institution, whether employed as a dry nurse or as a multitasking wetnurse for the children of the middle class. In fact, although the Brazilian census in 2000 showed the growing presence of women in the economically active population, this presence was concentrated in the domestic workforce. The gradual increase in domestic work leads to adult women's being replaced by young women as employers seek to keep these forms of work low-wage. This indicates the prevalence of 'historical continuities' in this type of work: the avoidance of investment in the social sector thanks to the persistence of 'invisible and cheap labor,' performed by women.[18] This 'historical continuity' is partly owing to the transition from unpaid work performed by enslaved women to unpaid (or badly paid) work performed by young women working as substitute mothers, with the emergence of a reproductive economy proper to domestic space.

According to the *Pesquisa Mensual de Empleo del Instituto Brasilero de Geografía y Estadística* (Monthly Employment Report of the Brazilian Institute for Geography and Statistics) for March 2006, domestic workers at this time represented 8.1% of the population employed in the six metropolitan regions covered by the report, which states: 'for historical and cultural reasons, this contingent of workers is predominantly made up of women (94.3%) and of black and brown [*pardo*] people (61.8%)'.[19] Among the women who make up 94.3% of this workforce, the majority are thus black or brown, the descendants of the wetnurses of old, who have become today's nannies.[20] These numbers hide the immense population of domestic workers who are not formally employed.

The Two Mothers in the Mirror of Myth

If double maternity is absent from academic research and interpretation, it is, by contrast, palpably present in Afro-Brazilian religion, which constitutes another hermeneutics, with other resources for symbolization, including a mythological vocabulary. My first encounter with a cryptic reference to this form of maternity happened in the bars in Recife, where I listened to the city's residents—*filhos de santo,* or saints' followers (literally, saints' children), who frequented *terreiros,* where rites are performed—as they passionately discussed a theme whose importance I couldn't quite understand. It struck me as funny that people would spend so much time and energy on discussions that lasted late into the night, on the relative importance and function of different kinds of waters: salt water from the ocean and fresh water or sweet water from rivers, waterfalls, and lakes. It was only later that I came to understand that these were conversations about two mothers, Oxum and Iemanjá, and about their two roles, their very different contributions to life, and the very different kinds of bonds that could be formed with each.

This interest in debating the role and relative importance of each of these mothers is probably due to the fact that a rare surviving fragment of a Yoruba myth is remembered by the practitioners of an orthodox and conservative Xangô cult in Recife.[21] And this is a myth about the separation of the waters precisely:

> There is no creation myth invoked except in references to a few fragments about the 'separation of the waters.' Some people mentioned these to me with the aim of contesting Iemanjá's (salt water's) supposedly higher status than Oxum (fresh water). Because she appeared first when the world began, Oxum is, by this account (but not in the dominant account), said to be older than Iemanjá and therefore higher in rank or status, although the latter is commonly thought to be her mother.[22]

In the mythological description of divinities, Iemanjá is what the cult's practitioners call the 'legitimate mother' of the Orixás, or gods. Here the biological mother—the mother who gave birth to the gods and goddesses who make up the pantheon—coincides with the juridical mother. In fact, unlike in the case of Trobriand paternity discussed above, here the *genetrix* and the juridical *mater* are one and the same: the phrase 'legitimate mother' points to the coincidence of these two functions. Still, there is a second form of motherhood—or rather a third, since it is added to these two, which from this mythological perspective are really one—for the cult's practitioners, who distinguish 'legitimate' motherhood from a form of *de facto* motherhood or motherhood in practice, which they call 'nurturing [*criadora*].' This is the motherhood represented by Oxum. In this context, it is common, as I have noted, for everyday conversations to touch on the difference between nurturing [*criar*] children, raising or caring for them or bringing them up, on the one hand, and, on the other, giving birth to them.

It is very common among the cult's practitioners—its 'people'—to give children to others to raise, or to receive them to raise. Here the circulation of children and the practice of raising children who are not one's own is the norm. Thus the contrast between the two kinds of mothers points to the historical and sociological divergence between the white mother living in the Casa Grande, or the big house, and the black nanny or wetnurse, who cares for this white mother's white and 'legitimate' children.[23] Though respected and opulently adorned, Iemanjá—whom I see as a palimpsestic figure for the former—is not the recipient of much sympathy from the faithful when they converse in the backrooms of houses of worship.

Iemanjá is described as cold, hierarchical, distant, and indifferent.[24] She is a mother in a conventional sense; that is, she mothers conventionally. Although she is tender in her appearance, people say that this tenderness is a matter of self-control and good manners rather than a matter of heart, compassion, or affection. It contrasts with the real affection offered by Oxum, the 'adoptive mother.'

As a divinity associated with the sea, Iemanjá is said to share its characteristics. She is 'traitorous' and 'false' like the ocean. This evokes the Atlantic Ocean's historical betrayal of the enslaved people brought to the New World, where the Atlantic stood between them and Africa, marking their insuperable distance from it. There is in this sense an ambivalence in people's relationships to the sea, which separated them from Africa in the past but in the present binds together the coasts of both continents. Iemanjá's 'falseness' is explicitly associated with the duplicitousness and unpredictability of the sea, whose surface hides its turbulent depths, which cannot be seen. This makes the emergence of a storm or tidal surge unpredictable: 'you see the surface, but you don't see the depths,' as the cult's practitioners say. In the practice of cowrie shell divination, Iemanjá, the 'legitimate,' biological, and hieratic mother 'speaks' from the two positions called *obedi* and *ossatunukó*. The first of these terms means 'betrayal'; the second, 'we see the surface but not the depths,' or, again, 'falseness.'

As I have tried to demonstrate elsewhere, the unpredictability of Iemanjá's character is also reflected in her iconic song, 'Okarilé'.[25] In this song, the inclusion of both binary and ternary beats—the alternation, that is, between four binary beats and three ternary beats—introduces a duplicity in the form of a cyclical jolt or shock in the tune's rhythm that can also be seen in the *orixá*'s dance during spirit possession, that is, when she 'comes down' to possess someone.

In the myth of the coronation of the kind of the *orixás* in the pantheon, Iemanjá—and not, as we might expect, the *orixás*' father, Orixalá—is the god that places the crown on the head of one of her children. According to the myth, when the day of the coronation finally arrived, everything was set up so that the firstborn and most responsible and industrious of her children, Ogum, would be crowned. But then Xangó, the youngest and his mother's favourite—described as spoiled, seductive, and ambitious—prepared a soporific potion that he then offered to Ogum, 'in his coffee.' After Ogum fell asleep, Xangó dressed himself in sheepskin so that he could pass himself off as his hairy older brother. (The hair covering Ogum's skin points to his primitive nature, his status as firstborn.) In this way, Xangó acceded to the throne. In the half-light required by ceremonial protocol, the coronation began. The aspect of the myth that 'saints' children' invariably underscore at this point is that, even before placing the crown on his head, Xangó's mother immediately perceived that one of her children had taken the place of the other, in other words, that the child on the thrown was not Ogum, who was meant to be there, but rather Xangó. The *filhos de santo* are emphatic and insist on noting that 'for Iemanjá the only thing that matters is avoiding anarchy at any cost.' For this reason, she proceeded with the coronation ceremony, crowning Xangó, the child who had managed to reach the throne and thus become king through deceit.

In the popular interpretation of this myth, Iemanjá allowed Xangó to take Ogum's place through the use of guile because—'as she always does'—she put her desire to maintain formal order before her commitment to truth and justice: 'Iemanjá doesn't want anything to disturb the social order. For this reason, even though she knew she was doing so, she crowned the wrong child.' Here the myth describes the foundation of a reign of injustice and favouritism, a reign of inequality presided over by Iemanjá. The rule of injustice is also foundational for history and the state, which must be preserved at any cost, whether or not it is sustained by the principles of justice. The acceptance of the unjust coronation represents nothing other than a recognition of the context in which slaves and descendants were forced to live. The 'legitimate mother,' the *mater* and *genetrix* in Brazil—as opposed to the mother who raises children—reproduces the harms of a false, a traitorous, and above all an unjust world. The myth is a page taken from social history.

In the doubling of Ogum and Xangó, we can find an echo of the doubling of Iemanjá and Oxum. But popular sympathies are not aligned with the hard-working and disciplined *orixá*, with the 'legitimate' firstborn, who is harmed and deprived of rites by his greedy brother. People instead sympathise with the younger brother whose demands were met because he resorted to guile, who usurped the crown and became king through cunning. People identify with this younger son because they know that his ways are the only ways to survive under a state whose laws do not serve the interests of justice but those of order. In this way, the myth points to the profound complexities of the collective psyche of those who were forcibly incorporated into the nation by the slave trade, only to then be kept in a position of economic and political marginalization by a complete lack of public policies capable of repairing their means of inclusion. By siding with the 'illegitimate,' people decide to speak through myths. And they celebrate the situation that led the 'legitimate mother,' too, to side finally with the illegitimate and irreverent king, the younger son who subverts the order of succession to the crown, 'out of her fear of anarchy.' It remains for us to find out whether this new king will transform the order that he has just entered or will be transformed by the protection that Iemanjá offers or the conditions of the inclusion that she imposes. 'Iemanjá protects the wrong son under her skirt,' people say.

Thus the political import of the myth is disclosed. Its cryptic statements point to the lie at the very foundation of the establishment and its laws. Although it speaks to a latent sense of ethical estrangement, the myth does not seek to formulate an alternative moral statute, but rather to produce a sociology, a hermeneutics adequate to the social context. Elsewhere I have called this a pragmatic psychology.[26] It is a manual for survival under an alien and arbitrary regime.

To sum up, then, in this religious 'codex,' the figure of the 'legitimate mother' refers to at least four problems that are of fundamental importance in this tradition. Each of these is charged with ambivalence: the separation from bonds of kinship and biological ties; the 'false' nature of the 'legitimate maternity' emblematised by the white matron in the slaveholding 'big house'; the sea's role in separating slaves from their origins in Africa; and the indifference and treacherousness of the state.[27] I have treated these problems and their interpretations exhaustively in earlier analyses.

The descriptions of the two mothers in this myth and in people's commentaries on it are not in keeping with the discourse of the white hygienists whom I mentioned earlier. Here we confront a bifurcation, one that remains difficult to locate because of the hegemonic power of the Brazilian nation. I am referring to a bifurcation between white speech and black speech in the historical record and in the register of the symbolic. For a wide range of reasons, it is not easy to locate this divergence between white speech and black speech in interviews or sociological studies conducted in the open, interviews or studies that ask respondents about the relative attributes of the two mothers. A hegemonic discourse whose purpose was and is to preach the culturalist (read: the 'fundamentalist') values of a nation that purports to be welcoming as well as all-encompassing—a discourse pioneered by the ideologically armed Arts and Sciences and spearheaded by authors like Gilberto Freyre and Sergio Buarque de Holanda—has effectively blocked the participation of subjects who are differently positioned and who seek to articulate this different positioning in their speech. This is not yet to mention hegemonic discourse's effect on all aspects of capitalist societies; such a discourse unifies the aspirations of subjects, and in this case makes it so that even mothers from the least advantaged social classes (including even women who practice Candomblé). These subjects avail themselves of a cryptic, encoded way of speaking, through the noble and potent forms of myth. Thus in the divergent voices of the hygienists, on the one hand, and Afro-Brazilian myth, on the other, we find the unmistakable traces of two subject positions, two contrasting views of the roles and values of the two mothers.

The Foreclosure of the Black Mother in White Discourse

The detailed hermeneutics of dual motherhood that we find in Afro-Brazilian myth contrasts with the absence, within white hermeneutics, of a figure of profound historical importance: the nanny. In my view, the double character of the maternal bond deserves to be inscribed more forcefully within the analysis of the psychic life of Brazilian society, since the phenomenon is not a trivial or inconsequential one. However, the academic racism enshrined in the country does not allow for such an inscription and has resulted in the implicit expulsion of any investigation of this kind.

I came face to face with this problem when, years ago, as a foreigner in Brazil and a mother to a young son, I visited the Imperial Palace in Petrópolis together with a group of colleagues who were also professors of anthropology.[28] On our journey, as we were discussing questions related to the social world around us, its customs and objects, I was taken by surprise and ended up separated from the group when I came across a small painting found in one of the salons, where it hung by itself above a piano and without any identifying labels (figure 1).

Figure 1

Anonymous
Nhozinho no colo da mucama [Little Boy on the Maid's Lap]

Oil on canvas, 0,55 x 0,44m

What struck me—to the point of overwhelming me—was how current the painting was, since it represented a scene that I saw every day in our house. Two bodies, with skin of contrasting colours, united in an embrace suggestive of an intense amorous seduction, an erotic bond between mother and child of the kind discussed by the first feminist theories of motherhood.[29] *A nanny and a child, yesterday and today,* I said to myself. The baby's pink hand rests confidently against the breast of the proud, young, black mother, who seems to show the world (and certainly the painter) the pride shown by all mothers as she offers the baby an enveloping, assured form of protection. I looked around the painting for a plaque or wall text that could bring me closer to a past that was so present. But I could find no such label.

It was only seven years later, in 1995, as I was leafing through old books on Brazilian history in the Latin American and Caribbean Collection at the University of Florida in Gainesville, searching for information on this image, that I again came across the at once surprising and familiar painting that I had seen that afternoon in Petrópolis. And this confirmed my first hunch. It was, in fact, according to the distinguished historian Pedro Calmon, a painting of 'D. Pedro II, a year and a half old, in his nurse's lap,' an oil painting by Jean-Baptiste Debret .[30] In a book published thirty-five years after Calmon's, in 1998, Lilia Moritz Schwarcz's *As barbas do imperador: Dom Pedro II, um monarca nos trópicos* (published in English as *The Emper-*

or's Beard: Dom Pedro II and the Tropical Monarchy of Brazil), a reproduction of the same painting appears, but without the identification provided by Calmon. The caption here introduces doubt, both by noting that the painting is only 'attributed to Debret' and by adding that 'some authors question the identity of the baby' and the other figure shown in the image, a '*mucama negra*,' 'a black maid' ('his black nanny' in the English translation).[31] Adopting the same attitude of uncertainty both with respect to the painter and with respect to the figures represented, the Imperial Museum in Petrópolis labelled it 'Anonymous. Maid with a Child in her Arms. Oil on canvas, unsigned.' That was the label that accompanied the image when this essay was first published. Today, the painting's official label takes even more distance from, and goes to greater lengths to evade, the African roots of the Brazilian emperor's upbringing. The text reads, 'Maid with a child in her arms. Oil on canvas, unsigned and undated,' and includes this note of explanation: 'This is a portrait of Luis Pereira de Carvalho, a young lord [*nhozinho*] at the breast of his maid Catarina.' But two clues prompt us to question this description: first, all non-religious paintings in the palace at Petrópolis are paintings of Dom Pedro or of the members of his immediate family; and second, the baby's strikingly wide forehead lets us glimpse the well-known face of the adult emperor, as shown in the numerous images of him that exist.

In opting for the description of the image offered by Calmon—who sees in it the representation of Dom Pedro de Alcántara as a baby in the arms of his wetnurse—I am also tempted to refer to Ernst Kantorowicz in order to suggest that the painting gives us a sense of the king's two bodies: the private and the public, where one hides the other.[32] Except that, in the painting, the private body and the public body appear in a state of confusion that excites the interpreter's imagination, even to extremes. With its pink, fleshy baby, grasping the black breast of the figure who completes his world—as if he wanted to become one with her—this small painting shows both a public and a private scene, a scene that is privately public.

We see a baby, who could be any baby, surprised and disturbed in an everyday Oedipal scene, perhaps while he is being slowly walked. We see the painter, with the Law that he introduces into this world not only as a subject, but in this case as a transcendent subject. And we see the nanny: the mother, Jocasta, who is black. The baby, interpellated and held up by his companion, hesitates to withdraw his hand from the mother's breast. The painting seems at once to be a painting of the baby and an allegory about Brazil, clinging to a mother-fatherland that has never been recognised but is not for all that any less real: Africa. It allows for a sort of transcendental comparison that lends the force of reality to all of the 'legitimate' babies in the nation who are in the process of being forcibly snatched from the warm arms or the laps of dark-skinned women, from the intimacy of their relations to black mothers, from their fusion with these mothers' bodies, which makes it impossible to distinguish in a lasting way between the 'I' and the 'you.'

But we should note something else as well: this process of detachment presages a profound loss: a double detachment that entails the sacrifice of the mother, her dark skin, and her native Africa all at once. This has distinctive implications for the emergence of the subject, who will then have to effect a double obliteration. The ferocity of this process will be inversely proportional to the attachment, the devotion, that was there in the beginning, at the start of this subject's life.

The non-white mother is torn away, and—although she will remain encrypted and encoded, as always, in psychic life—the possibility of naming or symbolizing her is hidden from view. Another figure is smuggled into her place, another scene that indefinitely postpones and thwarts the effort to rescue her or even recover the memory of her. Maria Elizabeth Ribeiro Careiro went in search of the nurses in the work of historians whose works are canonical and still widely read, including Gilberto Freyre, Caio Prado Júnior, and Emilia Viotti da Costa, among others. In these works, she found that the image of the black mother, of the wetnurse, was instrumentalised in narratives that ideologically 'soften' slavery in Brazil. Ribeiro Cairo writes:

> Now as a figure, the "black maid" is invoked as if she embodied and explained the various experiences of enslaved women who provided maternal care—experiences that were perhaps not always so good or so tender. Women robbed of their own forms of expression and politics, deprived of their own bodies and destinies even in Marxist discourse, reappear in a singular image, an image of what "softens" the blows dealt by life—by class, race, and ethnicity [...] The image of the black mother appears in the minefields of class conflicts as a figure redolent of delicacies, exuding warmth in the imaginary, lightening the burden and softening the yoke of slavery within social memory.[33]

If the nanny-mother's humanity is reaffirmed whenever she is hired, the image of the tender black mother and affectionate memories of her are used to minimise the violence of slavery. We thus confront a 'perfect crime' of the kind discussed by Jean Baudrillard: the outer elements of the scene persist like a kind of shell or skin, while its inner content and determining features are removed and surreptitiously replaced by others through a strategy of resemblance.[34]

The ignorance of this scene, the silence that suppresses it, the persistent invisibility of its tragic implications, and its literary transformation into an array of customs that are ultimately festive—all of these contrast with the exhaustive description of the comparable problems of *malinchismo* and repulsive origins that we find, across historical periods, in Mexico.[35] Attention to Mexican people's torturously ambivalent relationship to the maternal figure of La Malinche is a constant in Mexican historiography, anthropology, and vernacular culture. La Malinche was the Indian mother of the whole Mexican nation, an illegitimate concubine, a slave first of the Aztecs and later of the Spanish, and the lover of Hernán Cortés. Mother of all *hijos de la chingada* (sons of bitches, or more literally children of the raped, fucked, or beaten woman), she was raped and fertile. La Malinche was also the translator and traitor who moved between Spanish and the various indigenous languages of pre-Colombian Mexico. Mexicans see her and inscribe her within their history despite the ambivalence and the insecurity that results from their doing so: the perception that they are the illegitimate children of this union and copulation between two bloodlines that are antagonistic now as they were then.[36] They write this origin story into literature as the story of a foundational curse: the curse of La Malinche. In Mexico, there is thus a symbolization without mystification and without occlusion of the irreparable and undesirable aspects of the founding of the nation. The exercise of power and enforced submission are not spectacularised in scenes of enjoyment, and the rape that there was at the origin continues to disturb the present, remaining hateful and indefensible. Defeat and suffering are not overcome or ignored in favour of festivity in the work of Mexican essayists; their tragic dimension persists even in the stories told by liberal writers. Literary, historical, and anthropological strains of central national importance stage the ancestral collision between the public and private in a tragic key and not as a kind of Italian *commedia dell'arte.* [37]

By contrast, the suppression of this tragic scene in Brazil—or its erasure through romantic redoubling—reminds me of another scene that touches on this sore spot, this sense of *something that can only be seen from without,* a scene that involves three converging foreign gazes. I am thinking—following a kind of free association—of a story told by Nelson Rodrigues, who writes of Jean-Paul Sartre's visit to Brazil, together with Simone de Beauvoir, in 1960. As Rodrigues notes, Sartre was committed to the struggle for decolonization in Algeria and would later write a preface to Frantz Fanon's *The Wretched of the Earth* (1961). The elites of Rio de Janeiro who hosted Sartre—and whose encounters with him Rodrigues describes—must surely have reminded him of Fanon's earlier work, of Fanon before his coming to consciousness, of the Fanon who, in Martinique, still thought of himself as French:

Ah, Sartre! In his seminars the audience ate him up with its eyes. [...] Hearing him there, we must have seemed like three hundred old dogs. [...] He looked out at us as if we formed a horizon made up of cretins. [...] One night, there he was, with Simone de Beauvoir, his girlfriend, in the apartment of a colleague. He had the same disdain. He looked out at those present like someone who says, "What cretins! What imbeciles!" At a certain moment, the hostess came by to offer him some *jabuticabas*. Sartre started to eat them. But curiously he ate them with a certain sense of boredom (he wasn't far from finding them, too, cretins, imbeciles). Then, on his twentieth *jabuticaba,* he stopped and asked the question, with a certain irritation: "And the black people? Where are the black people?" The genius hadn't seen so much as a single mixed-race person at any of his seminars. Only blonde hair, only blue eyes, and, at the best of times, skin tanned at the beach. Lo and behold, Sartre faced the obvious. He repeated, after spitting out the pit of the *jabuticaba*: "Where are the black people?" At the window, one Brazilian whispered to another: "They're out there attacking a driver."

> Where are the black people? Here is the question that Brazilians should ask one another, even if they will not find the answer. There is no way to respond to the Frenchman's question. In fact, we do not know where the black people are. [...] Since I was a young man, however, I have felt black solitude. "Here is what I learned from Brazil: here white people don't like black people, and black people also don't like black people."[38]

Sartre's exclamation—'Where are the black people?'—is comparable to my own stupefied question: 'Where is the nanny?' I looked for her, for example, in the excellent anthology *Historia das mulheres no Brasil* (The History of Women in Brazil), and I didn't find her.[39] In this beautiful and important book, the word *babá* doesn't appear even once, despite the fact that it forms part of the conventional Portuguese vocabulary. The nanny or nurse is not discussed either in terms of her subjectivity or in terms of her social role. Still less is her presence investigated from the point of view of the children she raised or that of the 'legitimate' mothers who delegated to her such an important part of their maternal work. I cannot find a trace of this set of relationships. At best I find the category 'wetnurses' listed among the services provided by women. One reference on page 250: 'Slaves worked mainly in the fields, but they were also used by their masters as weavers, spinners, embroiderers, carpenters, oil vendors, wetnurses, pages, cooks, seamstresses, starchers, and laborers who provided all kinds of domestic service'.[40] The other appears on page 517: 'Statistics from the state of Rio Grande do Sul in 1900 show that around 42% of the economically active population was female [...] There is no shortage of examples of women workers: washerwomen, ironers, wetnurses, fortune-tellers'.[41] To be sure, the book does register the importance of the circulation of children and of forms of kinship not based on blood among the working classes, which I noted above in connection with my commentary on the myths of the Xangó cult in Recife, which I have also discussed at greater length elsewhere. 'If we want to reflect on motherhood in the working classes, we also need to account for the role of grandmothers, nurses, and adoptive mothers'.[42] But these acknowledgments always appear unaccompanied by specific analyses; the nurse or nanny always figures here as an item in a list.

Already in the twentieth century, it seems to me, the nanny's crucial function is caught in the blind spot left by the three female figures who do find their way into the historical record: the private-public mother whom Margareth Rago calls the 'civic mother,' the femme fatale, and the working woman who comes to form part of the 'productive' working classes, from which black people and especially black women are excluded.[43] What is foreclosed in the figure of the nanny is thus at once reproductive work and blackness. *This is a foreclosure, a disregard or non-knowledge, of the maternal and the racial at once, of blackness and the mother.*

One of the rare places where I found a recognition of this woman's presence and also an indication of the paradox and the complex of meanings that she represents was in a description that appears in the work of a historian of the feelings cultivated in response to the problem of race, a historian who has lived outside Brazil for some time now.[44] I am referring to Luiz Felipe De Alencastro, who comments on a photograph taken in Recife around 1860, an image that is also used as the cover of the second volume of the *Historia da vida privada no Brasil* (The History of Private Life in Brazil), edited by Alencastro. His epilogue on this photograph is precious, at once moving and beautiful. I am very sorry not to be able to reproduce it here in its entirety:

> The child came with his maid [...] and leaned against and held his nurse. He clung to her with both hands. He knew her scent, her skin, and her warmth so well. It was when he was carried by the nurse or she was beside his crib or he clung to her while nursing during the day or at night that his baby eyes took note of and began to gaze out on the world. In this way he cancelled out her space: she was a thing that belonged to him, whether out of love

> or because she was his property by right. [...] The mystery of this photograph, taken 130 years ago, still speaks to us. It is the image of a paradoxical but admissible union, a union based on present love and past violence. It was violence that split apart the soul of this slave, opening the affective space now being invaded by the child of her master. Almost all of Brazil fits into this photograph.[45]

The 'right' to 'property' that Alencastro names here is not only the master's right to the slave, but also the Oedipal sense that every child has in relation to the whole, indiscriminate territory that is the maternal-infantile body. This feeling—this territorial sense, this sense of property, of a claim to the mother's body as part of the child's own—is long-lasting and difficult to leave behind. It persists. The subject clings to it for a long time, including even after he has understood that the original territorial unity is nothing of the kind. Even when this sense of oneness has been lost, the feeling of property remains. What was one becomes the premise of the one's domination of the other. Anything that betrays or limits this domination is not welcome, and loving feelings are thus easily converted into anger when the subject confronts the loss of what he thought was his own. Add to this the fact that this maternal body is in fact one that is owned or hired, a body that is paid for in rent or in wages, and the relation of appropriation is redoubled, as are its psychic consequences. We can better understand how these difficulties are compounded if we remember that this substitute mother—a slave or a waged worker—even when she is emotionally invested in the bond that she is hired to have with the child, remains divided or 'split,' as Alencastro says, because she is conscious of a past—of slavery or of poverty—that left her with no choice. No matter how much love she may feel for the child, she will always know that she did not arrive at this love or form her bond with the child as a result of her own desires, but rather because she was coerced by the search for survival.

Asking that we indulge the exaggerations of his sources, Alencastro also notes that in 1845, in all the empire there were not five upper-class mothers, ten middle-class mothers, or twenty lower-class mothers who nursed their own children, since they were replaced by the enslaved or free women who were hired for this purpose. The situation changes somewhat beginning in 1850, when immigration from Portugal allows for the hiring of white nurses.[46] This substitution happens, as I have already noted, in the context of hygienic pressures to avoid contamination especially from Afro-descendant wetnurses. In Brazil, these pressures did not succeed in eradicating, as they did in Europe and the United States, the practice of transferred motherhood; they only introduced some changes and limits into this practice. Among these was the ability to rent the services of white wetnurses for those who have sufficient purchasing power: if a slave nanny was '*put up for hire* by her owner, a free woman would *put herself up for hire*'.[47]

The objectification of the maternal body—whether the body of an enslaved or of a free woman, of a white woman or of a black woman—is delineated here: slavery and motherhood are shown to be proximate; they blur together in the gestures of nursing and the market for milk, where the free breast is offered up as an object for rent, a tool for hire. 'Mercenary' motherhood is here comparable to sexuality in the context of prostitution, and this has a decisive effect on the infant's psychic life, its perception of the feminine and non-white body.

The search for wetnurses for affluent families ends up pointing to another superimposition as well. Milk and blood both come to function as figures for heredity.

> *O Constitucional*, a São Paulo newspaper, explained in 1853: "The infant nursed with the mercenary milk of an African, will during his early development learn and imitate the customs and habits of its nurse, and lo and behold by the age of puberty, like other inhabitants of central Africa, he speaks a tainted language, using the strangest words as language."[48]

What the source claims here makes a lot of sense: a child breastfed or simply cared for from a young age by a nurse with darker skin, a nurse descended from enslaved Africans, will have incorporated this image as its own. *Even in the relatively rare case in which the last three generations of its ancestors do not have mestizo features, a white child will thus also be black by virtue of its originary fusion with or impregnation by the maternal body, perceived as part of the territory of its own body.* In the language of biology, we could say that its 'imprinting' will be black. In the diatribes that protest against the 'mercenary milk' that they think contaminates the benign, 'free milk' given by the biological mother, we can recognise more than the voice of the hygienist. Modernization in this context involved a 'racial animus against black people'.[49] The discourse of modernisation and racism were thus interconnected; they came together to oppose an enemy in Brazil who impregnated white ontology from within, even from within the space of psychic interiority.[50]

The Oedipal bond in breastfeeding, even when it does not involve a blood relation between mother and child, is thematised in different cultures. As Gilza Sandre-Pereira claims:

> Milk is, like other bodily substances, powerfully endowed with symbolic significance in various cultures, and breastfeeding is thus clearly more than a matter of biology and nutrition [...] Even when breastfeeding is not understood as a means of generating relations of kinship—

> which would in and of itself occasion sexual prohibitions—the relationship between semen and milk is at the origin of sexual prohibitions in many modern societies.[51]

Sandre-Pereira cites Freud in order to emphasise the erotic dimension of breastfeeding:

> No one who has seen a baby sinking back satiated from the breast and falling asleep with flushed cheeks and a blissful smile can escape the reflection that this picture persists as a prototype of the expression of sexual satisfaction in later life.[52]

Thus we can recognise kinship at the breast—later transformed into kinship on the lap and at the bottle—and the black ancestry to which this form of kinship gives rise, for both white and black people in postcolonial societies like Brazil's. The initial bonds of nursing and the intimacy of the relationship that gave these bonds historical continuity lend particular features to the emergence of subjects cared for in this way. In this case, the loss of the maternal body, or symbolic castration in the Lacanian sense, decisively connects the maternal relation to racial relations, and the denial of the mother to the denial of race and the difficulties of its symbolisation. Motherhood is thus infiltrated by a form of raciality, and raciality is infiltrated by motherhood. The sign of race and the sign of maternal femininity feed into one another. Thus, far from saying, like those who seek to romanticise this formative encounter, that the white baby's being cared for by a dark-skinned mother figure leads to a harmonious form of multiracialism, or that this is a matter of intimate interracial coexistence, *I am arguing, on the contrary, that racism and misogyny in Brazil are interconnected, brought together in a single psychic gesture.*

If we consider this scene from the perspective of the critique of coloniality, we can see that the introduction of hygienist discourse in Brazil reinforces and redoubles this psychic gesture. Brought to Brazil by doctors and pedagogues, this discourse took advantage of the modern and Western position, the exteriority of the hygienists, in order to create distance from what they perceive as the affective and cultural contamination coming from Africa. Thus modern hygiene offers the possibility of an external gaze, alienating the members of an elite that was seeking just such an exit. The foreclosure of the race embodied by the mother figure is fundamentally this: a symptom of adherence to colonial modernity.[53] Historical changes in the forms used to portray children from good families offer a perfect allegory for this process, which culminates in the forceful imposition of the hygienic and racist gaze on a peripheral modernity, and the suppression of the figure of the non-white mother. Rafaela Andrade Deiab analysed the sudden transformation in the photographic depiction of children with their nannies in the photographs taken by Miltão de Azevedo in his São Paulo studio between 1862 and 1885. Until roughly 1880, these photographs showed children in compositions that were modelled on the international styles of the period, except that in Brazil the typical European mother holding her child up to her face is replaced by the black nanny, who occupies the mother's position. Andrade Deiab explains this pose by noting that photographic negatives were not as sensitive then, and so photographs involved long exposure times during which the child would have to remain immobile: 'since the babies were more used to these women, their presence diminished the risk that the babies would grow restless while they were being photographed'. The mother's substitution by the nanny thus showed that children were more intimate with and trusting of their nannies, who were the only ones capable of keeping the children calm for the time it took to take the photograph. However, around 1880, Andrade Deiab says, photographic compositions begin to pay more attention to hiding the figure of the black nurse, even while the nurse is still necessarily there to hold the baby in her arms so that it can be photographed:

> Black nurses come to exist in photographs only as traces, in the form of a hand or a fist, before they are then completely expelled from the images [...] At first, they were shown with pride, with their whole faces visible. Later these faces were hidden or relegated to the background, out of

> focus or retouched to the point that they were completely withdrawn from the picture of the nation. But even covered over they remained; their work was enshrined in custom for three centuries.[54]

Andrade Deiab's article includes a striking photograph that shows a blonde baby held above what appears to be a dark cloak, under which one hand can barely be glimpsed, holding the small body, while another squeezes the child's small hand to comfort it as it faces the threat of the intrusive camera. But nothing can be seen beneath the cloth, and the outlines of the hidden nanny can only be inferred from the folds of the fabric. This is the perfect emblem for the nanny's absence in national memory: a cloak of forgetting covers over both the mother figure and her race. Race and motherhood are blanketed, and in their place we find only the void of foreclosure, which displaces an intolerable reality.

Like me, Jurandir Freire Costa points to the silence that, within psychoanalysis, surrounds the form of violence that we call racism:

> When we think of Brazilian psychoanalysis, of how it affects us, of how it has coexisted with so many 'peacetime crimes,' adopting an attitude of complicity or complacency or, at best, indifference, we should also ask ourselves another question: Which psychoanalysis is this? What kinds of psychoanalysts are we?[55]

Freire Costa approaches the problem that I have sketched here, without giving this problem the name of the wetnurse or nanny. For him, racism is a form of violence inflicted against the body and against the body's role in acting as a support for identity: '*the ideology of color* is in fact a front for a more damaging ideology: *the ideology of the body*'; 'the black subject, by repudiating its color, radically repudiates its body'. 'The persecutory relationship with its own body exposes the subject to a mental tension whose outcome is, as we might expect, the effort to eliminate the epicenter of this conflict'; 'the black subject, possessed by an ideal of whitening, is forced to seek the destruction of the traces of color on its own body and in its descendants'.

But it seems to me that Freire Costa stops short of completing this analysis when he locates its centre in the black subject itself as the bearer of the symptom. This symptom also belongs to many whitened subjects, those considered non-black, in Brazilian society. Clearly, in its emergence, the subject must leave behind the mother figure and her blackness in a single movement. This is true no matter the subject's colour and whether the mother figure's blackness is in the present or in the genealogy of slavery that still leaves its trace within the care for hire performed in the present. The fact that the mother is impregnated by this genealogy, which connects the enslaved woman's breast in the past to the lap that is for hire today, makes it impossible for this loss to be simply cut off from discourse or repressed. The suppression should be understood as nothing more and nothing less than a *disregard* or non-knowledge. The absence of knowledge of what bearing the mark of black motherhood entails, what a terrible destiny it is—this very absence is a technique of alienation and dispossession, a means of seeking refuge when faced with the possibility of recognizing oneself as in fact an inheritor of this slave lineage, even when one is 'white'. Unfortunately, the use of this technique does not go unpunished; it is not free but comes at a cost.

'The traumatic repetition of what has been foreclosed from contemporary life threatens the "I,"' according to Judith Butler.[56] Butler, using the term 'foreclosure' in a distinctive and somewhat flexible sense, distinguishes between the negation or repression of a desire that once existed, and the 'preemptive' foreclosure or expulsion of the very possibility of a desire; that is, a desire that is anticipated and preemptively expelled in advance, before an attachment to it can be experienced.[57] The mechanism of foreclosure is thus, for Butler, what allows for the anticipation and prevention of certain affective entanglements. The negation brought about through foreclosure is more radical than the negation brought about by repression. If the latter involves cutting a given thing off, foreclosure is matter of absence rather than inscription. But this absence determines one's defective entry into the *symbolic*, in other words, one's loyalty to an inadequate symbolization that leads to collapse when the *real* irrupts, that is, when one is confronted with what cannot be contained or organised.

In Brazil, debates in the present show us that some sectors of the country's illustrious elite continue to resist the recognition of a subject who is differently positioned, a black subject who speaks of blackness and of black people's differential place in Brazilian society. By negating this claim to speech, by seeking to prevent these subjects from speaking, the members of Brazil's elite can be seen to show us the founding impossibility of inscribing the mother's blackness in discourse. The racist certainly loved and—why not?—still loves his dark nanny. Except that he cannot recognise her race or its consequences for his own subjectivity. If she were suddenly to appear on the scene and remind him of their kinship, he would respond with uncontrollable virulence. *I am thus referring to a kinship that cannot be named either as one's own or as someone else's.*

If this is what is seen as absent from the child's point of view, from the *other* mother's point of view, or what Afro-Brazilian religion would call the 'legitimate mother's' point of view, there is something else that should be said. This 'civic mother'—that is, the educating mother whom Margareth Rago describes, the mother defined by hegemonic bourgeois thought and the tenets of modernity—will have to embody *the paternal function*, at least in part. That is, she will have to incorporate the law and block the child's intimacy with the nanny. This mother's *paternal* function within the familial scene can also be recognised in the fact that, by denying the nanny's maternal bond with the child—by replacing an affective with a contractual relation—the 'legitimate mother' remains imprisoned within a masculinist and misogynist logic that removes the nanny-mother from humanity, transforming her into an object to be bought and sold.[58]

Each society has its own form of racism. As I have argued elsewhere, I believe that in Brazil the cognitive operations of expulsion, exclusion, and violence are not brought to bear on 'other' people. Instead these operations arise from a structure that is lodged within the subject's interior, implanted there at the very origin of the subject's emergence.

Notes

1 Special thanks to Jocelina Laura de Carvalho, Carlos Enrique Siqueira, Claudia Maia, Emilio García Méndez, Ernesto Ignacio de Carvalho, Maria Elizabeth Carneiro, Ondina Pena Pereira, Tania Mara Campos de Almeida, Tiago Amaral, and everyone who, from the time when I first began to ruminate (or reflect, think, or meditate) about this text in 1988, told me stories about nurses that helped me to compose this text. The text was translated into Spanish by Clarisa Corral, with revisions by María Luisa Femenías.

2 Bronislaw Malinowski, *The Father in Primitive Psychology* [1927] (New York: W. W. Norton & Company, 1966) pp.14-15.

3 See John A. Barnes, 'Physical and Social Facts in Anthropology', *Philosophy of Science*, vol. 31, no. 3 (July 1964) 294–297.

4 See Ernest Jones, 'Mother-Right and the Sexual Ignorance of Savages', *International Journal of Psycho-Analysis*, vol. VI, no. 2 (1925) 109–130; and Bronislaw Malinowski, *Sex and Repression in Savage Society* [1927], in *Collected Works*, vol. IV (New York: Routledge, 2013).

5 See Melford E. Spiro, 'Virgin Birth, Parthenogenesis and Physiological Paternity: An Essay in Cultural Interpretation', *Man,* vol. 3, no. 2 (1968) 242–261.

6 See Edmund Leach, 'Virgin Birth: The Henry Myers Lecture, 1966', *Proceedings of the Royal Anthropological Institute of Great Britain and Ireland* (1966); and Edmund Leach and others, 'Virgin Birth', *Man,* vol. 3, no. 4 (1968) 655–656.

7 Spiro, op cit .

8 Melford E. Spiro, *Oedipus in the Trobriands* (Chicago: University of Chicago Press, 1982) p.61.

9 One of the few texts that I know that addresses this problem is by Luiz Tarlei de Aragão, who, however, offers an analysis that shares little with the analysis that I develop here. See Luiz Tarlei de Aragão, 'Mère noire, tristesse blanche', *Le discours psychanalytique—revue de l'Association Freudienne,* vol. 4 (1990) 47–65.

10 In Brazilian anthropological literature, there are examples of analyses of the psyche in societies in which, as in Brazil, the maternal function is divided between a number mothers; see, for instance, Stanley N. Kurtz, *All the Mothers Are One: Hindu India and the*

Cultural Reshaping of Psychoanalysis (New York: Columbia University Press, 1992).

11 Suely Gomes Costa, 'Proteção social, maternidade transferida e lutas pela saúde reprodutiva', *Revista de Estudos Feministas*, vol. 10, no. 2 (2002) 301–323 (p.305).

12 Gilza Sandre-Pereira, 'Amamentação e Sexualidade', *Revista de Estudos Feministas* vol. 11, no. 2 (2003) 467-491 (pp.473-474).

13 Sandra Lauderdale Graham, *House and Street: The Domestic World of Servants and Masters in Nineteenth-Century Rio de Janeiro* (Austin: University of Texas Press, 1992) p.118.

14 ibid. This aspect of the process of modernisation has correlates in other Latin American countries. See, for instance, the excellent studies of the hygienic persecution of wet-nurses in Peru: Claudia Rosas Lauro, 'Madre sólo hay una. Ilustración, maternidad y medicina en el Perú del siglo XVIII', *Anuario de Estudios Americanos*, vol. 61, no. 1 (2004) 103-138; and Margarita Zegarra, 'La construcción de la madre y de la familia sentimental. Una visión del tema a través del Mercurio Peruano', *Histórica*, vol. XXV, no. 1 (Lima: 2001) 161–207.

15 See Joaquim Manoel de Macedo, *As Víti-mas-Algozes* [1869] (Rio de Janeiro: Typografia Americana, 1991).

16 See Maria Vitória Pardal Civiletti, 'O cuidado às crianças pequenas no Brasil Escravista', *Cadernos de Pesquisa*, no. 76 (São Paulo: February, 1991) 31-40.

17 See ibid.; and Elizabeth K. C. Magalhães and Sonia Maria Giacomini, 'A escrava ama-de-leite: anjo ou demônio?', in *Mulher, mulheres*, ed. by Carmen Barroso and Albertina de Oliveira Costa (São Paulo: Cortez/Fundação Carlos Chagas, 1983) pp. 73–88.

18 Gomes Costa, op cit . p.307.

19 Instituto Brasileiro de Geografia e Estatística - IBGE, *Perfil dos Trabalhadores Domésticos nas Seis Regiões Metropolitanas Investigadas pela Pesquisa Mensal de Emprego (Recife, Salvador, Belo Horizonte, Rio De Janeiro, São Paulo e Porto Alegre)* (Brasília: Indicadores IBGE, 2006) p.3.

20 For the figures on domestic work, see also Rita Laura Segato and Laura Jimena Ordóñez, *Mulher negra = sujeito de direitos e as Convenções para a Eliminação da Discriminação* (Brasília: AGENDE - Ações em Gênero, Cidadania e Desenvolvimento/ UNIFEM/ SEPPIR, 2006).

21 I am referring to the myth's historical persistence, as opposed to other myths' recent recovery through formal or informal research.

22 Rita Laura Segato, 'Yemanjá e seus filhos: Fragmentos de um discurso político para compreender o Brasil' [1995], in *Santos e Daimones: O politeísmo Brasileiro e a tradição arquetipal* (Brasília: Editora da Universidade de Brasília, 2005) p.570.

23 See Rita Laura Segato, 'Inventando a Natureza: Família, sexo e gênero no Xangô de Recife' [1995], in ibid. (translated as Rita Segato, 'La Invención de la Naturaleza. Familia, Sexo y Género en el Xangó de Recife', in *La nación y sus otros: Raza, etnicidad y diversidad religiosa en tiempos de políticas de la identidad* (Buenos Aires: Prometeo, 2007).

24 See *Santos e Daimones.*

25 See Rita Laura Segato, 'Okarilé: Yemoja's Icon Tune', *Latin American Music Review,* vol. 14, no. 1 (1993) 1–19.

26 See Rita Laura Segato, 'Cidadania: Por que Não? Estado e Sociedade no Brasil à Luz de um Discurso Religioso Afro-Brasileiro', *Dados: Revista de Ciencias Sociais,* vol. 38 no.3 (November, 1995). (Also in Rita Laura Segato,

La nación y sus otros: Raza, etnicidad y diversidad religiosa en tiempos de políticas de la identidad (Buenos Aires: Prometeo, 2007).)

27 I have called the set of figures and problems that recur in accounts of the interactions among the divinities in this pantheon the 'Afro-Brazilian religious codex' (see Rita Laura Segato, 'The Color-blind Subject of Myth; or, Where to find Africa in the Nation', *Annual Review of Anthropology*, vol. 27 (1998)). These figures and problems can also be seen in the patterns of social interaction, the ritual practices, and in the informal conversations among the cult's practitioners. As in Mexican codices, and despite the fact that these are pictorial records, whereas the tradition that I am discussing here is mainly an oral tradition, encoding or codification results from the repetition and consistent reuse of a set of figures or motifs. What results is a philosophical codex, in which the principles of a worldview are insistently repeated, to the point that it is possible to identify the basic patterns and shared ideas that form the basis of the mythology, the ritual forms, and the social life—that is, the *civilizing discourse*—of the Afro-Brazilian religions, *their historical projects*. I have called this oral text a 'codex' because of the stability and coherence of the characters and patterns of meanings that it comprises.

28 These colleagues were Otávio Velho, Luiz Eduardo Soares, Rubem César Fernández, and José Jorge de Carvalho.

29 See Nancy Friday, *My Mother/My Self: The Daughter's Search for Identity* [1977] (New York: Delta, 1997).

30 See Pedro Calmon, *História do Brasil: Século XIX – Conclusão, O Império e a Ordem Liberal* [1955], vol. V (Rio de Janeiro: Livraria José Olympio Editora, 1963) 2 edn.

31 Lilia Moritz Schwarcz, *As barbas do imperador - Dom Pedro II, um monarca nos trópicos* (São Paulo: Companhia das Letras, 1998) p.26.

32 See Ernst Hartwig Kantorowicz, *The King's Two Bodies: A Study in Medieval Political Theology* [1957] (Princeton, NJ: Princeton University Press, 2015).

33 Maria Elizabeth Ribeiro Carneiro, 'Procuram-se Amas-de-Leite na Historiografia da Escravidão: da "Suavidade do Leite Preto" ao "Fardo" dos Homens Brancos', *Em Tempo de Histórias*, vol. 5, no. 5 (2001) pp.44-45.

34 See Jean Baudrillard, *The Perfect Crime* [1995], trans. by Chris Turner (London: Verso, 2008).

35 I am referring to the work of elaboration of customs undertaken by Gilberto Freyre, whose work also sought to digest what had not yet been digested by the Brazilian nation.

36 See Sandra Messinger Cypess, *La Malinche in Mexican Literature: From History to Myth* (Austin: University of Texas Press, 1991).

37 See Roger Bartra, *La Jaula de la Melancolía: Identidad y Metamorfosis del Mexicano* (Mexico: Editorial Grijalbo, 1987); Carlos Fuentes, *El espejo enterrado* (Mexico: Aguilar, 1992); and Octavio Paz, 1994 (1950), 'Los Hijos de la Malinche' [1950], in *El laberinto de la soledad* (Mexico: Fondo de Cultura Económica, 1994); among others.

38 Nelson Rodrigues, *O Óbvio Ululante: Primeiras Confissões* (São Paulo: Companhia das Letras, 1993). See also Jean-Paul Sartre, 'Préface', in Frantz Fanon, *Les damnés de la terre* (Paris: Seuil, 1961).

39 See *História das Mulheres no Brasil*, ed. by Mary del Priore (São Paulo: Contexto, 2006).

40 Miridan Knox Falci, 'Mulheres do sertão nordestino', in ibid. p.250.

41 Claudia Fonseca, 'Ser mulher, mãe e pobre', in ibid. p.517.

42 See ibid. pp.535–539; and this problem also appears in Renato Pinto Venâncio, 'Maternidade negada', in ibid. p.202

43 See Margareth Rago, 'Trabalho feminino e sexualidade', in ibid. p.92.

44 Luiz Felipe de Alencastro has lived in France, where he currently teaches, from 1966 to 1986, and again from 1999 to the present. See Luiz Felipe de Alencastro, 'Interview with Cibele Barbosa and Eliana Bueno-Ribeiro: 'Passages de Paris'', *Revue Scientifique de l'Association de Chercheurs et Etudiants Brésiliens en France*, no. 1 (April, 2005). http://www.apebfr.org/passagesdeparis/edition1/entrevista.html.

45 Luiz Felipe de Alencastro, 'Epílogo', in *História da Vida Privada no Brasil 2: Império: a corte e a modernidade nacional* (São Paulo: Companhia das Letras, 1998) pp.439-440.

46 See Luiz Felipe de Alencastro, 'Vida Privada e ordem privada no Império', in ibid. p.63.

47 ibid. p.64.

48 ibid. p.65, quoting *O Constitucional*, 07/05/1853, p.3.

49 ibid. p.66.

50 See José Jorge Carvalho, 1988, 'Mestiçagem e Segregação', *Humanidades*, nol. 5, no. 17 (1988); and Segato, 'The Color-blind Subject of Myth'.

51 Sandre-Pereira, 'Amamentação e Sexualidade', pp.471-472. It is surprising to note that in this article Sandre-Pereira uses the discrediting phrase 'mercenary wetnurses,' with apparent tranquillity. This phrase belongs to the vocabulary of the misogynist hygienists, but she reproduces it several times in her text without offering any commentary or critique. See also: https://www.youtube.com/watch?v=cmbrArDpSq8.

52 Sigmund Freud, *Three Essays on the Theory of Sexuality* [1905], trans. by James Strachey, in *The Standard Edition of the Complete Psychological Works of Sigmund Freud, Volume VII (1901-1905):* A Case of Hysteria, Three Essays on Sexuality *and Other Works*, ed. by James Strachey, with Anna Freud, assisted by Alix Strachey and Alan Tyson, 24 vols (London: Vintage, 2001) VII, p.182.

53 See the essays ‘Gender and Coloniality: From Communitarian to Colonial Modern Patriarchy’ and ‘Sex and the Norm: On the State-Corporate-Media-Christian Front’, in Rita Segato, *The Critique of Coloniality: Eight Essays*, trans. by Ramsey McGlazer (Abingdon: Routledge, 2022), on the exteriority of the colonial gaze and its analogy with the scientific and pornographic gazes.

54 Rafaela de Andrade Deiab, ‘A memória afetiva da Escravidão’, *Revista de História da Biblioteca Nacional*, vol. 1, no. 4 (October 2005) 36-40 (p.40).

55 This and the following quotations are all from Jurandir Freire Costa, ‘Da cor ao corpo: a violência do racismo’, in *Violência e Psicanálise*, (Rio de Janeiro: Graal, 1984) pp.107-108.

56 Judith Butler, *The Psychic Life of Power* (Stanford, CA: Stanford University Press, 1997) p.9.

57 ibid. p.23.

58 I am grateful to Jocelina Laura de Carvalho for offering me a first glimpse of this idea.

www.ingramcontent.com/pod-product-compliance
Ingram Content Group UK Ltd.
Pitfield, Milton Keynes, MK11 3LW, UK
UKHW041143300926
15471UKWH00012B/118

9 781919 601960